PRAISE FOR *LIVING MINDFULLY*

"Simple, direct, and full of real-world wisdom, this book is for everyone interested in bringing mindful awareness into their daily lives."—Susan Kaiser Greenland, author of *The Mindful Child*

"Engaging and accessible, *Living Mindfully* is a wonderful introduction to a most beneficial approach to living a life. Reading the book is like being on retreat with a wise and practical teacher." —Kathleen Dowling Singh, author of *The Grace in Aging*

"While many mindfulness books stop at providing instructions for general practice, *Living Mindfully* takes the essential next step of providing clear guidance in how to apply mindfulness directly to the vital areas of our lives, such as relationships, work, parenting, and heartbreak. The author's heartfelt wisdom gently guides readers to use their newly developed skills in these contexts to enhance their lives."—Lizabeth Roemer, PhD, coauthor of *The Mindful Way Through Anxiety*

LIVING MINDFULLY

AT HOME, AT WORK,
AND IN THE WORLD

living
mindfully

at home, at work,
and in the world

Deborah Schoeberlein David, MEd

with David Panakkal, MD

Wisdom

Wisdom Publications
199 Elm Street
Somerville, MA 02144 USA
wisdompubs.org

Library of Congress Cataloging-in-Publication Data
David, Deborah Schoeberlein, author.
  Living mindfully : at home, at work, and in the world / Deborah Schoeberlein David,
M.Ed. ; with David Panakkal, M.D.
     pages cm
  Includes bibliographical references.
  ISBN 1-61429-153-5 (pbk. : alk. paper)—ISBN 978-1-61429-171-8 (Ebook)
  1. Meditation—Buddhism. I. Title.
  BQ5612.D38 2015
  294.3'444—dc23
                                  2015008733

ISBN 978-1-61429-1-534   ebook ISBN 978-1-61429-1-718

19 18 17 16 15
5 4 3 2 1

Cover design by Laura Shaw Design, Inc. Cover illustration by Allison Meierding.
Interior design by Gopa & Ted2, Inc. Set in Granjon LT Std. 11.4/14.8.

Wisdom Publications' books are printed on acid-free paper and meet
the guidelines for permanence and durability of the Production Guidelines
for Book Longevity of the Council on Library Resources.

This book was produced with environmental mindfulness. We have elected
to print this title on 30% PCW recycled paper. As a result, we have saved the
following resources: 16 trees, 7 million BTUs of energy, 1,379 lbs. of greenhouse gases,
7,478 gallons of water, and 500 lbs. of solid waste. For more information,
please visit our website, wisdompubs.org.

Printed in the United States of America.

FSC
www.fsc.org

MIX
Paper from
responsible sources
FSC® C011935

Please visit fscus.org.

For Our Parents
and Our Children

Table of Contents

List of Exercises

1 • Mindfulness: You and I

THIS IS A HANDBOOK for experiential learning and an invitation to enrich your life. It maps the landscape of "why" mindfulness works, "how" to practice meditation, and "what" living with mindfulness can mean—for you personally, professionally, and in relationships. Once you begin training your brain, you will experience benefits that include sharper thinking, deeper awareness, improved emotional resilience, and better physical health. The following chapters combine practical and personal information, along with instructions and examples, to provide companionship for an ongoing journey—yours.

My husband, David, and I wrote this book together, although for the sake of simplicity, my voice predominates. I am a teacher by calling, a writer by trade, and a woman with the roles of daughter, wife, and mother. He is a psychiatrist as well as former medical school professor, US Army officer, and US diplomat. His clinical work has spanned the globe. We both practice meditation privately and frequently collaborate to provide mindfulness training professionally.

In the first few chapters of this book, I share some of my own experiences with mindfulness, not because they are somehow more deserving of attention than another person's, but because they are what I know intimately. These snapshots from my story invite you to consider your own unique narrative. I hope that you find benefit in the techniques that have been my ballast across the seas of life.

Together, we explore how mindfulness practice can help you pass safely and successfully through the milestones of a modern life. Sometimes in my own life, I thought for sure my ship was going down, but mindfulness helped me survive the desperation and sinking feelings without losing hope. At other times, the wind and waves let me soar with exhilaration, yet even from these heights, watching my mind brought me back safely to earth. Always, the practice of mindfulness was the steady wind that moved me forward, battered or joyous, fragile or strong.

Life is full of choices, and the experience of recognizing, considering, making, and then living with our choices requires courage—lots of it. When we're lucky, we can choose the best of several acceptable options or make a clear-cut decision between good and bad. Sometimes we're less lucky and there are only undesirable possibilities that force a choice between something bad and something that's even worse. And of course, the more significant the life choice, the greater the risks and rewards.

Managing and making choices, fully cognizant of their implications, is courageous. But even more so is recognizing that sometimes the only real choice available pertains to *how we live* with the people, circumstances, and things we cannot change. Consider: if you dislike your job, the obvious next step is to find a new one. However, many of us are "stuck" in an unfulfilling job or unpleasant workplace environment because of practical considerations such as health insurance, the need for steady income, or simply the absence of viable alternatives. Then what? When you can't change the external realties (your job), the only available option is to work with your inner experience. Perhaps you can focus on the satisfaction you receive from helping new employees gain competence. The bottom line is this: whether or not we can alter external circumstances, living with mindfulness helps us know where we are and supports us through the process of finding our way.

WHAT IS MINDFULNESS?

Mindfulness practice is a practical and secular form of meditation. According to modern research, mindfulness techniques train your brain to function in ways that make your life easier, healthier, and more enjoyable. I'm not saying that mindfulness directly alters the (sometimes incredibly hard) facts of life, but rather that living mindfully facilitates experiencing reality more comfortably and constructively.

Mindfulness practices exercise the brain in much the same manner as physical activity hones muscle; in both cases, training fosters fitness. Mindfulness is not brainwashing, and it won't make you "zone out" or escape life. The opposite is true: practicing these techniques day-to-day increases your alertness, concentration, and engagement right here, right now. Mindful living is about feeling truly alive.

Meditation is both a mental practice (the process) and a state-of-mind (the outcome). Unlike most conventional scenarios in which process precedes outcome, with meditation *the process is the outcome*— both develop in tandem. As you become more experienced, the practice will become easier and the results will simultaneously become richer.

The practice of mindfulness is a calling, like the practice of medicine. A young doctor is no less a physician than another with a lifetime of experience. But technical expertise, like wisdom, deepens with years of practice. Likewise, a beginner's practice of mindfulness is no less authentic than a master's, although the nature of their skills and insights would likely differ.

Mindfulness is a particular form of meditation that involves paying attention to what's happening in and around you, right here and right now. Practicing it improves your mental efficiency as well as the depth and speed at which you process information. Furthermore, meditation improves mental stability by improving your ability to place your attention at will and sustain your focus. Thus, becoming mindful allows you to experience your life fully so that it doesn't just pass by.

In addition, your coping skills will improve as will your ability to manage stress and mitigate the negative aspects of life. Even better, the practice enhances the desirable experiences of life—emotions such as joy and curiosity; the physical pleasure that comes with exercise, good food, or sex; and the satisfaction and intimacy of healthy and happy relationships.

The essential progression of mindfulness practice is very simple and incredibly powerful: you train your attention and awareness so that you think better, feel better, and increasingly give others the best of yourself. After all, the gift of total attention is the ultimate expression of love. Beyond the necessities of survival, attention is the most precious commodity we can offer our family, friends, and community and even our work, hobbies, or civic duty. Being "there" with or for someone involves having the skills and intention to be truly "here" with them.

And being "here" is the key to living more fully *and more ethically* in the present, which translates into having a more meaningful and fulfilling life day by day. Believing that enhancing your own experience is the ultimate measure of mindfulness practice is a fundamental and grave misunderstanding. Sure, mindfulness is a personal practice, but it matters immensely in community. The more mindful you become, the greater your capacity to live ethically and precisely—because you're paying close attention. Without mindfulness, we are oblivious. With mindfulness, we can make active and constructive choices. Either way, we're accountable for what we do—and how we live.

There are many reasons that you might be interested in mindfulness. Perhaps you need an effective approach for managing physical pain or reducing your stress. Maybe you're looking for research-based techniques that improve your brainpower at work or which demonstrate psychological benefits in the treatment of anxiety or depression. Or perhaps you just want to enhance your everyday experience so that the daily grind becomes more pleasurable and fulfilling. Regardless of your motivation, the basic practice of mindfulness is the same, and as you'll see in this book, the approach is practical, accessible, and best of all feasible for busy twenty-first-century people like us.

I embarked on my own experiment with mindfulness a dozen years ago because I desperately wanted to find another, better, way to experience daily life, and I'd run out of other options. My circumstances were sufficiently difficult to motivate me to learn and practice something different. "Maybe, just maybe," I thought, "mindfulness will help me become more balanced, happier, and more productive." I didn't have a whole lot of faith that it would work, but since meditation didn't seem to have a major downside, I opted in and hoped for the best. To my amazement, the experiment was a success. Mindfulness practice improved the quality of my life almost immediately and continues to do so.

My experiment continues—as does my skepticism. Since mindfulness enhances my daily experience, I continue to practice even as I keep my mind and my eyes wide open. There's nothing mystical or magical underpinning my commitment—just common sense. As long as the discipline of training my mind enhances the freedom I feel (especially from unhealthy thoughts and emotions), I happily submit to a modest mental training routine. I take it day by day. But over the years, I've come to realize that applying mindfulness in the present actually fuels my motivation for living mindfully in the future—practicing makes me want to practice more. It's a gift that keeps on giving.

WHERE I BEGAN

Historically, mindfulness meditation has roots in ancient Buddhist practices. Buddhism is a religious tradition, however, and the ethics supported by mindfulness practice are universally accepted across wisdom traditions. I've met mindfulness practitioners from many diverse religious traditions, and we all seem to have a common experience: mindfulness meditation complements the cultural legacy of different birth traditions and enriches varied spiritual paths.

I began learning about Buddhism in my teens, when I began looking beyond the highly intellectual and fiercely proud strain of Conservative Judaism in which I was raised. My childhood experience of being Jewish was complicated and largely unsatisfying. I loved the majesty of the High Holy Day services and the warmth of my grandmother's Shabbat candles. But I couldn't connect with the austerity of the synagogue services or the Zionist orientation of Hebrew school and Jewish youth groups.

I wanted to celebrate the magical legacy of a five-thousand-year-old tradition but felt constrained and oppressed by the undercurrent of anti-assimilation. I was drawn to the mysticism of Kabbalah but couldn't wrap my head around the restrictions of Orthodoxy. Granted,

I was an intense child, and my spiritual calling was a little unusual, but I understood perfectly by high school that I wanted a spiritual path and would have to look beyond Judaism to find it.

In college, I began meditating. My first formal experiences were at a Zen Buddhist monastery that operated in Bar Harbor, Maine, during the 1980s. The monks and nuns in residence were a familiar mix of counterculture spiritual seekers and hippies. Like me, they were products of mainstream American upbringings. Also like me, they were looking for something to explain their experiences and some way to live with greater ease. Sitting together, in the silent half-light of dawn and dusk, offered a possible path to finding answers and at least provided some solace and community. For the first time, I felt accepted in my search.

After a few weeks, I made an appointment with the abbot for a formal interview session. When I entered the small room, I found him sitting on a cushion, just as I expected, with a serene expression, gentle eyes, a shaved head, and formal Zen robes. But what I hadn't expected was the realization that despite his authentic training and Zen lineage, his cultural heritage was just like mine: he'd started out a "nice Jewish boy from New York." I nearly choked, almost forgot what I was supposed to do, and then decided that I wasn't going to do it.

"I can't bow to you," I told him, "it's not what Jewish people do." He laughed and said he was quite aware of that. Then he asked me to specify what element of bowing posed the greatest obstacle. No problem. I knew just what to say. "Well," I explained, "I can't bow to a person." So he stood up and stepped out of my line of vision. "And," I continued, "I can't bow to a representational statue, such as the Buddha, because Jews don't worship idols." No problem. He simply picked up the statue of the Buddha that was in front of me and placed it to the side.

I'd run out of excuses and didn't know what to do next. He kindly gave me a hint: "Do you think you might feel comfortable just bowing, you know, toward whatever is divine within you?" I thought about that proposition; after all, Jews do ritually bend our knees in reverence on certain occasions. "Okay," I replied, "but how exactly do I bow?"

He showed me a traditional Zen bow that brings the forehead in contact with the ground; since it looked like a familiar yoga posture, I decided to try bowing then and there.

Something shattered inside me, like the burst of ice with the rush of thawing water, and I sobbed uncontrollably when my head came down. I was totally unprepared for that rush of emotion and sense of release. I'd never known the freedom that comes with surrender, especially when the surrender is to the divine. It was pivotal moment, and I realized in the clarity that comes with such experience that my beliefs had kept me tightly bound and that working with my mind could set me free. When I asked the abbot how to work with my thoughts and feelings, his answer was radically simple yet completely unexotic: "You meditate."

I have, on and off, ever since.

WHERE YOU CAN BEGIN: JUST ONE BREATH

The only way to gain a real understanding of mindfulness—or any other form of meditation—is through direct experience and personal practice. It's not enough solely to think or read about it. Of course, having a conceptual foundation is important, but there's more to mindfulness than knowledge and analysis. If you're ready, you can begin right now.

Take one Mindful Breath:

- Just breathe *in* and then breathe *out*.
- Pay attention to taking that breath.

That's all.

Taking this single Mindful Breath might seem ridiculously simple, but actually there's a lot going on. The most obvious effects are physiological. When you take that one purposeful breath, your body relaxes. Maybe only just a little; after all, a single breath is very brief. But still, even one breath can make a difference.

Try again now, and take another Mindful Breath. Then reflect on how your body feels. You might even take a third Mindful Breath. Has your body relaxed a little more deeply with each inhalation-exhalation cycle? Once again, take a Mindful Breath and notice whether any tension in your muscles lessens, even just a little bit.

Taking one Mindful Breath after another can seem artificial, even uncomfortable, because you're paying attention to a body function that's familiar and unremarkable. We breathe every minute of our lives; so long as you are living, your breathing is adequate. However, we usually only notice the experience of breathing when something is wrong or difficult. You were breathing continuously while reading this chapter, but you probably didn't really think about breathing until this section. Then, if you took advantage of the prompts, you focused in an unusual manner on a usual action.

At the simplest level, the difference between a Mindful Breath and normal breathing is that applying mindfulness enables you to notice the breath *as it moves*, in the present moment. There's nothing fancy about this, but the experience of paying attention to breathing is a kind of visceral epiphany. When I first began practicing mindfulness, I realized that I'd failed to recognize the most essential experience of being alive. Breathing was so familiar, so close, and so necessary that I'd somehow never noticed it.

I wondered what else—what other experiences—might come into focus with greater mindfulness.

WHEN STRESSED, BREATHE

The essential difference between taking a Mindful Breath and simply taking a deep relaxing breath lies in the direct engagement of your attention.

You've taken deep breaths in the past and likely noticed the calming effects associated with doing so. While deep breathing relaxes the body, it doesn't automatically shift your attention onto the quality of your current experience. You can breath deeply while feeling stressed, while thinking, talking, walking, or doing just about anything else with your body and mind. In contrast, taking a Mindful Breath engages your brain in focusing on the experience of breathing. You might still be in a stressful situation or doing something else (like walking), but your attention shifts toward the task of taking a Mindful Breath. Put simply, the key is experiencing the act of breathing *while you do it*.

There are many benefits to shifting attention and awareness to experiencing whatever you're doing, not the least of which is that you shift your attention and awareness *away* from something else. This is particularly useful for managing—if not reducing—stress.

Stress is the body's physiological response to threat, and it happens when we encounter a "stressor" that triggers the sympathetic nervous system. Stressors can be external (for example, a dangerous event) or internal (a strong emotion like anger or fear). Although people's stressors differ, we share the experience of stress and the associated cascade of physical and mental changes.

Stressors cause the more primitive part of the brain to release stress hormones that launch a series of automatic physiological changes known as the "fight-or-flight response." These changes include increased heart rate, muscle tone, blood pressure, and concentration/focus. When stressed, you maintain this heightened state until the danger passes and your brain returns your body to a resting state.

Usually, the surge of stress hormones subsides when the stressor passes. This works best when the stressor involves an external threat, such as an oncoming car. If you have to jump out of the way to avoid being run over, a fight or flight response can save your life. Then, once you make that rapid movement and reach the safety of the curb, your brain will trigger your return to a resting state. Likewise, you might feel stressed before making an important presentation at work, but the stress will likely begin to lessen as soon as you feel more confident or when the presentation is done. This kind of stress is normal and can actually enhance your performance; it's also fairly benign because it passes relatively quickly.

The problem is that most of us regularly experience a very different—and unhealthy—type of stress: one that causes anxiety and from which there is little, if any, opportunity for rest or recovery. This type of stress occurs when you have relentless demands in the workplace or relationship difficulties at home. Under these circumstances, you are constantly in a state of fight or flight. This is chronic stress, and the delayed (or absent) return to the resting state has both short- and long-term negative impacts on cognitive functioning, emotion regulation, and physical health. The good news, however, is that mindfulness practice can help mitigate these effects.

When you take a Mindful Breath, you purposefully counter the fight-or-flight response by enhancing the system responsible for returning the body to a resting state. When something stressful happens, your body naturally starts climbing up the stress ladder. Then, when you take that Mindful Breath, you pause on that ladder (even if only for a few seconds), and this brief rest helps slow everything down. Therefore, even if your stress level continues to rise during an ongoing situation, it would likely increase less dramatically than it would have done otherwise. The more often you pause, the lower your level of stress will be, and the clearer your mind.

Staying low (or at least lower) on the stress ladder increases the likelihood that you'll have a balanced response to the situation. Most of us tend to react fast and furiously when something happens that triggers an intense, particularly negative, emotion. Later, we often regret our knee-jerk reactions, thinking, "If only I'd waited…." Taking a Mindful Breath buys you time so that the "thinking" part of your brain can catch up with the "emotional" part, priming you to refocus more clearly and make better decisions.

Think about the familiar encouragement to "take a deep breath when you're upset." Unfortunately, hearing someone say this in the midst of a stressful situation can be downright annoying. As a result, "taking a deep breath" may well increase your stress, rather than help it dissipate. This is normal; it's very hard to switch your attention to taking a Mindful Breath when your emotions are already engaged and your body is aroused with the stress response.

Proactive training is best; learning to take Mindful Breaths in normal conditions, when you're less stressed, prepares your brain and body to taking one spontaneously during a crisis or when you are under duress. Training your mind with more comprehensive mindful breathing techniques (as introduced in the subsequent chapters) provides even greater familiarity and skill. The routine of practicing mindfulness will also help you actually remember to take a Mindful Breath when you really need it most. Purposefully taking a Mindful Breath is even more powerful than spontaneously taking one.

But I'm getting ahead of myself. For now, just consider that although Mindful Breath yields benefits immediately, the results are even greater when you have a stronger foundation in mindfulness practice overall.

Adding "In" vs. Adding "On"

In the rush of modern life, many of us get up most mornings and hit the ground running. There are perhaps kids to care for and send off to school, chores to do, a partner to nurture and enjoy, a job to be done, and, if we're lucky, time for exercise or recreation or socializing before we fall into bed exhausted. Each day is full, full, full.

Before I learned to take a Mindful Breath, I'd usually reach bedtime still trying to wrap my mind around what happened earlier in the day. Trying to keep everything in place was like holding a long unwieldy strand of beads that overflowed my fingers and dangled from my hands. On a good day, I could stay reasonably calm and place the string carefully to the side. I'd feel a comfortable closure to the day and look forward to a little intimacy and affection—or, more likely and just as precious, a good night's sleep. But when I was tired or frazzled or inattentive, I'd drop the thread and watch the pearls scatter. In other words, I'd lose my composure and the consequences would ripple across my family, into my bed, and through the long hours of thrashing, wishing for sleep.

Now I still end up with a long string of beads at the end of day, but I have a significantly different experience because I breathe, purposefully, all along the way. Each conscious Mindful Breath functions like a little knot tied between the beads. Maybe your grandmother had an old-fashioned pearl necklace with tiny knots that separated the lustrous beads. If so, the knots had several functions: they protected the pearls from grinding and chaffing against each other, they created space between the pearls so the light could reflect their loveliness more effectively and catch your eye, and they also created "stoppers" so that a broken string only resulted in the loss of one or two pearls. These knots made the necklace stronger, more attractive, and more resilient. Pausing between events, tasks, or emotional episodes works exactly the same way.

Bookends are another applicable analogy. Bookends are simply objects that keep a row of books standing tall rather than falling over with their accumulated pressure and weight. Pausing before and after a meeting, or before and after getting the kids breakfast and onto the school bus, or at either end of any other activity, helps contain the experience. These bookends mark the start and end of any given task and allow you to focus on that particular experience *in that moment* and then set it aside as you move into the next activity.

Taking a Mindful Breath when you engage in particular activities during the day helps you view the practice not as "adding on" to your tasks, but rather as "adding in" to already established routines. For instance, you might take a Mindful Breath with the following activities:

- Before answering the phone.
- While waiting for your computer to boot.
- While walking to the bathroom/to get coffee.
- Before and after meetings.
- Before responding to challenging emails, verbal statements, etc.
- Before drinking or eating.
- When you wake up in the morning or before going to sleep at night.

As you train in pausing, the technique will become increasingly familiar and easier to apply under duress. When a specific task or activity doesn't work well, you can consciously shift your attention to breathing and center yourself again. With a little practice, you're likely to notice that you take a Mindful Breath spontaneously when circumstances are particularly difficult.

Likewise, you might also naturally take a Mindful Breath when an event or experience goes really well to savor the experience and smooth the transition to whatever is next. Pausing won't cause you to lose touch with what happened during any given episode, but it will help you move forward into the next event freshly. If something critical happened that requires your attention later, you'll remember it and return your focus to that event when you have the time and the benefit of a clearer mind.

Taking a Mindful Breath might be a new technique for you, but no doubt, you've taken a special type of breath naturally in response to significant events in daily life. For example, sharing a moment of silence involves taking a collective and formal pause to mark the most serious, emotionally loaded, events. When you pause in a moment of silence, you participate in present-moment experience with a community. You focus your attention, as the larger group does collectively, on a particular person, object, or event. Then, as the moment stretches, you monitor your attention to notice if you become distracted so you can refocus in deference to the solemnity of the situation. In these moments, you pause and breathe to attention, just as a soldier salutes and stands at attention.

Moments of silence often acknowledge the presence of tragedy. This makes sense since the experience of extreme grief is simply too intense, individually or societally, to survive without making time to rest and reflect. People know this intuitively, and we've developed cultural rituals that foster pausing to better cope with pain and care for each other. In this context, pausing helps you manage your emotions in order to survive them and positions you to engage in constructive action despite the challenge of circumstance. But, as with applying any skill under duress, it's easier and more effective to take a Mindful Breath if you already know how.

A Mindful Breath is a mini-mindfulness technique that yields immediate benefits and even greater results with practice. The technique is feasible, even for the busiest people; all it takes is a little bit of effort and patience. As you'll see in chapter 2, Mindful Breath is the foundation of Pause, an even more practical mini-mindfulness technique, which—in turn—leads to more sophisticated mindfulness practices tailored for ordinary people like us.

Learning to breath mindfully, and practicing day by day, can enhance the quality of your life, just as it has mine. Similarly, pausing regularly will strengthen your ability to cope with extreme circumstances and contribute more effectively whenever others need your attention. It's easy to think that self-help and personal growth are self-centered endeavors, but in fact, taking care of yourself is the foundation of being able to care for other people. Learning to take a Mindful Breath is personal, but the impact of pausing—at the right time and place—can be infinite.

2 • Why Meditate?

MEDITATION IS FULL of paradox: it's a rigorous discipline that gives you limitless mental freedom.

At times, it can be incredibly boring, but coming to terms with that tedium actually primes your mind to recognize flashes of insight. Learning to meditate involves reducing external distractions in order to heighten sensitivity to inner distraction—it helps you develop greater skill and ease in working with the mind. Unfortunately, although meditation facilitates recognizing life choices, many of us wait to begin the practice until we feel that there's nothing else left to try.

Although I began meditating first during college, I avoided sitting still to look at my mind regularly for more than a decade. Then, in my mid-thirties, I returned to meditation when I realized that I needed a successful strategy for improving the quality of my life. Something healthy, which would profoundly and sustainably trigger positive change.

I wasn't even unhappy or bored in the conventional sense. I was simply unsettled and profoundly unsatisfied with my conventional life. I had two kids under the age of three, a full-time job in the non-profit sector (which was immensely satisfying but hardly lucrative) and at least several extra pounds around my middle that everyone told me "had to come off." My ex-husband was a fine man and a good father, but not my soul mate. I also had a difficult relationship with my mother and primary responsibility for an elderly grandmother who was ending her days nearby in a nursing home. Luckily, I had three tremendous assets: the unwavering support of my father, a brother I adored, and a deep belief that things could be better.

I had a lot to handle, but so did other people, and unlike me, they seemed to manage fine and enjoy life. So I followed their example and pursued all sorts of socially acceptable potential remedies to feeling crappy. I worked out, on and off, and socialized. I even mixed the two: taking power walks with a girlfriend while actively engaging in therapeutic venting. My approach was healthy, but it provided temporary relief, at best. I needed something stronger.

Fortunately, I already knew enough to stay away from the more common unhealthy strategies for coping with malaise. I wasn't interested in the dullness that comes with self-medicating by alcohol, pot, or pills. Neither did I have any interest in distracting myself by extreme physical training (I'm not marathon material) or becoming totally immersed in the sort of undoubtedly valuable and people-oriented volunteer opportunities (such as helping out at school or donating time to a local charity) that seemed to entice some of my more social friends. By the time I reached thirty-five, I'd run out of obvious options and began to have an inkling that I needed to try something radical.

After all, I couldn't seem to think my way out of my silent, subtle, and insidious misery. I wondered if, maybe, I was stuck in some kind of cognitive warp, if my mind was somehow chasing its own tail. I realized that I spent an awful lot of time thinking about my unhappiness, which made me feel even unhappier. So maybe the content of my thoughts was problematic, but so too was the way in which I was actually thinking. What if thinking wasn't the way to transformation?

There was only one way to find out, so I took the plunge and headed off to a Tibetan Buddhist meditation class advertised outside a coffee shop in the little rural Colorado town where I lived at that time. Worst-case scenario, I could always leave. After all, I had only the hour to lose.

ORDINARY PEOPLE, LOOKING FOR CHANGE

There was a lot that I liked about my first meditation class: the late afternoon sun streaming through the windows, the relative quiet of a room full of attentive adults, and more than anything else, the sense that I had company in my search for change. The room was full of other apparently ordinary people, some of whom I knew from the community, and all of whom at least seemed to be living examples of stability. Unlike my experience at the Zen monastery, there was nothing countercultural about the participants in this meditation class—although, perhaps, there were other "sleepers" like me in the group.

After introducing himself, the teacher made a statement that resonated with me. He said, "If you're here, it's probably because you're looking for something that you don't already feel you have. This is the right place if that 'thing' isn't an object at all, but rather a quality like contentment, or a longing for spiritual fulfillment, or the skills to manage your stress. Meditation helps many people find these 'things,' but the only way to know if practicing meditation can help you is to participate in a grand experiment with your mind."

Then he got tough. He explained that he would teach us how to meditate according to the teachings of an authentic Tibetan Buddhist lineage, and he told us that learning the practice is an opportunity deserving of respect and commitment. He challenged us to consider our intentions and make a choice: "Stay for the class if you'd like to learn how to meditate and are willing to practice fifteen minutes each day for a month; otherwise, don't waste your or our time." The bottom line was simple, he said, "If, at the end of that month, life is easier, you'll want to continue with the practice." If life isn't easier, he continued, "You'll know that this strategy isn't the right one for you, and you can keep looking—just as you are now, only with the knowledge that this approach didn't work."

I liked the simplicity and directness of his approach, and I've always been curious about experiments. This one seemed manageable; it offered low risks and high potential rewards. Fifteen minutes a day. Every day for one month. Either it would help—and wouldn't that be nice?—or it wouldn't, and the modest cost in time and energy was worth the gamble. Of course, there was a financial cost too. But the suggested donation was reasonable and seemed only fair. Along with others in the room, I was watching out for gimmicks or a con, but I felt he was trustworthy. After all, I could fully understand his motivation: he wanted to teach others about the spiritual path that had changed his life.

Today, I recognize that my desire to share what's worked so well for me is reminiscent of my teacher's own motivation. This book is very much rooted in what I learned—and what I continue to learn—during the "grand experiment" he spoke of. The funny thing is that the terms of the basic proposition are the same whether you hear them, as I did, from a teacher or read them, as you are, right now. The fact that you're reading this chapter suggests that you're interested in learning more, but are you willing to give the practice its due?

If you experimented with taking a Mindful Breath in chapter 1, you have an initial sense of whether you liked the feeling of mental rest and physical relaxation that comes with quiet, purposeful breathing. While taking a Mindful Breath provides a valuable and practical mini-mindfulness break, the only way to develop confidence that meditation can make a real difference in the quality of your daily experience is to learn, experientially, through more formal meditation. For that, you need to practice at least a few minutes a day, most days, for a few weeks or a month.

There's no shortcut, and practicing meditation does require effort. Consider it an investment in your mind. And, as smart investors know, it's important to do a little background research before you commit time and energy. That's why the next section explains how using your mind to meditate actually benefits your brain.

BUZZING IN THE BRAIN

Let's start by considering the difference between the brain and the mind. Although this is not a hardcore scientific definition, the term "mind" often refers to the experience of human consciousness; the mind is the intangible experience of "being." The brain, in contrast, is the tangible organ, located within the skull that supports consciousness and controls the physiological processes that make life possible.

Although the brain is a hugely complicated organ, you don't need to be a scientist to understand what it does. Imagine that the skull is like a domed room, round on the ceiling and edges. The room is packed full of kites layered in all directions from top to bottom and side to side. Each diamond-shaped kite has frayed ribbons on its corners and a single long string that falls toward the floor. Some kites touch the ceiling, whereas others are barely off the floor, and the many-stranded ribbons from each kite touch their neighbors. As the long strings fall toward the floor, strands branch out, bundling together to form increasingly thick cords.

In this analogy, the kites, including their ribbons and strings, represent neurons. Neurons communicate by sending electrical signals that trigger the flow of chemicals crossing the spaces between cells. Imagine that each kite is electrically charged, able to receive and send sparks of energy to other kites constantly. Some energy signals, aptly named "excitatory," trigger more excitement in other neurons, triggering chain reactions of activity. Others signals are "inhibitory" and communicate instructions to return cells to a resting state. Regardless, communication between neurons in the brain and the rest of the body is constant; it's the nature of life. We literally buzz with energy, and the more efficiently our neurons pass their messages, the better our performance.

One of the most exciting scientific discoveries of the twentieth century is neuroplasticity, a term that refers to the "plastic" or changeable quality of neurons. In the past, people thought the brain was a fixed structure and that once a neuron died, it was lost forever. According to the old view: If you were lucky, you got a good brain that worked well and made you smart and healthy; if not, well... you were stuck. Fortunately, we were wrong; the brain is a dynamic organ that is able to change and regenerate.

Meditation leads to desirable changes in the brain that strengthen neural connections to support paying attention, applying awareness, and even cultivating empathy and compassion. The more you use the neural connections associated with these skills, the greater the efficiency of energy transfer among the cells. Connections that are regularly activated become energy highways, whereas rarely used connections retain the character of small rough roads. Meditation exercises and impacts neural connections that actually change the brain.

However, these desirable changes only occur with actual practice. For that, you need some basic instructions. The good news is that meditation starts simple, and the details accumulate only as you gain greater understanding and find further areas for exploration. So it's time to build on the Mindful Breath technique from chapter 1 and learn to use Pause, a more sophisticated mini-mindfulness break that includes the three core steps of all mindfulness techniques.

PAUSE

We are about to go beyond the basic explanation of why taking a Mindful Breath helps you slow down, if not reverse, the stress response and explore *how* this happens. As presented in chapter 1, taking a Mindful Breath involves one straightforward action: simply experience the act of breathing while you take one breath. But what's actually happening is far more complicated, as you'll see through the progression of the next few paragraphs.

To begin, read and then follow the three steps below.

- Focus your attention on taking a single, full breath.
- Take the breath.
- Return your focus to the book.

These three steps prioritize the mental skill of paying attention. Attention is like a laser beam, and right now your attention is illuminating these words and ideas. When you take a Mindful Breath, you purposefully place the beam of your attention onto the natural experience of breathing, which orients your mind onto the current moment.

The task of taking a Mindful Breath precludes thinking about anything else—past or future. You need to stay in the present, and that's the whole point. Let's do this one more time:

- Focus on taking a single, full breath.
- Take a breath.
- Return your focus to the book.

Although we've highlighted the role of attention, another mental skill is equally essential to taking a Mindful Breath: awareness. Awareness enables you to notice if/when the beam of your attention moves somewhere else or loses strength and clarity. With awareness, you know whether you're truly "here" now by observing whether you stay focused during the Mindful Breath or if your mind wanders elsewhere.

Compared with paying attention, the task of deepening awareness is somewhat more difficult for most of us, perhaps because modern education and workplace activities prioritize paying attention to *something* (an object) without giving any importance to the quality of attention or the experience of paying attention. As a result, we don't ordinarily realize that focusing on an object isn't the same thing as *noticing the act of focusing*. In the context of mindfulness, awareness is about monitoring attention.

Put differently, attention and awareness are two sides of the same coin. Attention allows you to focus, sharply, on an object of your choice. Awareness enables you to witness what happens with your attention. They work together to keep you focused, which includes recognizing if/when you become distracted and need to refocus once again.

Once you understand how attention and awareness work together to support mindfulness, the more general experience of taking a Mindful Breath gains greater detail. This more specific technique is called Pause, and it contains explicit direction regarding the three core steps of all mindfulness practice: focus, observe, and refocus. Here are the instructions for **Pause**:

- **Focus** on taking a single, full, breath. (Attention)
- **Observe** if/when you lose focus on that (Awareness)
  single, full breath.
- **Refocus**, if needed. (Attention)

When you Pause, you run your brain through a training routine. The act of placing your attention, voluntarily, and maintaining your chosen focus during the course of a breath actively engages your pre-frontal cortex. This is the part of the brain that allows you to selectively pay attention at will: choose the object of attention (in this case, your breath), block out distractions (such as this book and whatever else is happening in and around you), and maintain focus (despite competing demands for your attention). It's also the brain region that allows you to witness your own experience. This, in turn, enables you to refocus when and if necessary.

Please bear in mind that while Pause is a more advanced practice than a Mindful Breath, honing your attention and awareness skills with any given technique is far more important than "advancing" to another. Experiencing *total presence* is the essential experience of mindfulness. Each and every technique in this book can facilitate this.

Just to reiterate: mindfulness is about strengthening the quality of your attention and awareness to become fully present with present-moment experience. You can use whichever techniques are most helpful in this process. The measure of your success is *your experience with mindfulness* not whether you use a "more advanced" technique.

When to Pause

The more you apply Pause, the easier and more effective the technique becomes. But knowing how to Pause for a breath is only part of this particular mindfulness practice. Another aspect is *remembering to do so*. In fact, using Pause and remembering to use Pause both involve the same three steps: focus, observe, and refocus. The main difference is the object of attention. While practicing Pause, you focus on your breath. But when the task is remembering to use Pause, you place your attention on recognizing when to apply the technique in real time—and then doing so. The same skills apply equally to using Pause so as to stay present and remaining sufficiently present in order to remember to use Pause.

Pause provides a kind of mental companionship. I feel more secure in my day since I know that Pause helps me, regardless of circumstances. Applying Pause reduces the tedium of the same old chores or the unpleasantness of doing things I dislike. Mindfulness won't make me like cleaning my house, or preparing my taxes, but nourishing my mind and body with Pause does help me feel better in the process.

Using Pause certainly enhances my experience of delight and pleasure. When I use Pause while eating chocolate, I savor the flavor more and have more time to enjoy it. Similarly, Pause helps me stay present when I play with my kids or spend time with loved ones. As a result, I enjoy the time together much more fully and am less likely to become distracted by chores or the constant pinging of technology. When I practice Pause in the midst of graduations and weddings, I come into more direct contact with my joy and rejoicing.

Likewise, when things are rough, using Pause helps me manage. When my kids or other loved ones tell me something I don't want to hear, I use Pause to get through the instant flash of unhappiness. I use Pause when I learn of unexpected expenses, and when I receive other types of unwanted news. Pause helps when I long for sunshine but get constant rain. The practice can't make the sun come out on a dark wet day, but it does help me find other sources of light and warmth.

Pause also helps when life seems utterly devoid of light, such as when searing pain—either emotional or physical—paralyses me. Sometimes there's absolutely nothing to say or do that can make a situation better, and all that's left is staying present (which is hard enough). When this happens, I use Pause and rely on my breathing an as anchor that keeps me from drifting toward the falls. Then, eventually, the pain lifts a little, and I'm still breathing.

Although our lives are unique and the world is replete with diversity, humans seem to share at least some common feelings and experiences. The rhythm of our days and nights are not so very different as to be utterly unrecognizable across the lines of culture, religion, ethnicity, race, or gender. We live in the same basic body (regardless of sex) and all have the same basic needs. As humans, we eat and feel hunger, we experience physical pain and total ecstasy, we think and we feel. The opportunities for using Pause are endless, and it's up to each of us to apply the technique when it suits us best. However, the following suggestions might help get you started.

Pause During an Ordinary Day

- When you wake up and begin to become aware of the day.
- When you're just about ready to get out of bed. If you're not really awake until you get some caffeine, use Pause as you savor that first cup of coffee.
- When you take a shower and breathe in the hot, humid environment.
- When you step outside and breath in the air at different times during the day.
- When you're about to eat, while you eat, or after you eat.
- When you speak with others.
- When you hear silence.

You get the idea: use Pause to facilitate being present with the myriad ordinary experiences of daily life; doing so brings freshness to the most familiar routines.

Pause When You Feel Wonderful

- When you enjoy the objects of sensation: taste, smell, sight, sound, and touch.
- When you experience pleasure while exercising, dancing, or making love.
- When you relish your favorite flavors.
- When you see beauty in your environment.
- When you experience pleasurable emotions, such as pride and satisfaction in a task well done.
- When you savor having a heart brimming with love.
- When you feel gratitude.
- When you find relief.
- When you celebrate.

Keep in mind that cherished moments are precious but all too often compromised by distraction. Treasure these times for their sweetness, *in the moment*, by using Pause.

Pause When You Feel Terrible

- When you fill with anger, fear, frustration, disappointment, grief, disgust, or dislike.
- When you notice that your stomach or throat tightens, and you feel like you can't get enough breath because your emotions are so intense.
- When you burn with the heat of hatred.
- When you can't think rationally.
- When you need to strategize about next steps.
- When you're totally stressed out.
- When you experience fury and want to lash out with violence (in any way).
- When you fail a test.
- When you lose a job.
- When you miss an opportunity.
- When you reach the end of a relationship.
- When you hear something horrible or heartbreaking.

Using Pause when life is hard brings physiological benefits and supports emotional resilience. Unwelcome news is stressful, and knee-jerk reactions often exacerbate the associated difficulties. Pause won't make bad news better, but it can help you handle difficulties more constructively and with less damage.

Pause When There's Nothing Else to Do

- When you experience excruciating pain.
- When you have no more words to say.
- When you learn that your beloved is leaving you.
- When you receive a dire diagnosis.
- When a loved one dies.

- When you grieve with a loved one who is ravaged by pain.
- When you lose something you cherish.
- When you suffer utter betrayal.
- When you question your faith.
- When you prepare for your own death.

Sometimes all you can do is manage each moment, one by one. In these instances, time changes pace and survival (physical and/or emotional) takes precedence. You need to keep breathing, although even that can require extreme effort. Using Pause supports that most fundamental of actions and makes hope possible.

KEEP ON BREATHING

I had a neighbor years ago whose no-nonsense words sometimes left me feeling bruised. She was nothing if not practical, and she accepted that life yields all sorts of experiences, much as the sea tosses everything from treasure to detritus on the beach. Her motto was "you get what you get, and you don't throw a fit." My initial reaction was "ouch."

Later, I realized she was right. Throwing a fit rarely helps, and we do get what we get—which is not always what we want or expect. Nevertheless, the motto can be off-putting and counterproductive.

I'd rather live by words that offer a constructive alternative to "throwing a fit." And I believe that we can have experiences that are not predestined by "what we get." I don't want to live at the mercy of things beyond my control, be they external forces, other people, or my own ignorance and emotions. I realize, of course, that I can't control all aspects of my life and world, but I can learn to manage my response and reaction to my life and world. I want to know what's real, now, in this moment, and I want to learn how to experience reality in ways that make "throwing a fit" irrelevant.

I'm not anywhere close to there yet. But using Pause led me to a new technique: Mindful Breathing, which has changed my life profoundly. Mindful Breathing is an important foundational practice that supports all types of meditation. You'll learn this particular technique in the next chapter. Following that, you'll see how Mindful Breathing provides a basic template for bringing mindfulness to thoughts, feelings, and physical sensations. The point at which I began practicing with Mindful Breathing was my first significant milestone. From there, the route of regular mindfulness practice continues to bring me a little closer to living fully day by day—through fully experiencing my life.

3 · There's More to Mindful Breathing

IF YOU'VE EXPERIMENTED with the mini-mindfulness breaks described in chapters 1 and 2, you already have a sense of how mindfulness practice can make a positive difference in your quality of life. The simple act of taking a purposeful breath can offer immediate relief, like a glass of cold water on a hot day. But an occasional break hardly satisfies a deep and lasting thirst, especially when you're in a lasting heat wave of stress, anxiety, or pain. If you crave more than temporary respite, you'll need more than mini-mindfulness techniques.

In other words, practice mindfulness the way an athlete stays fit: daily and with purpose and reasonable discipline. Following a specific training program, with clear directions and explanations, is essential. You are preparing for a special sort of marathon, while already running the course.

Runners, like mindfulness practitioners, push their bodies and their minds. They need good form, so their bodies move correctly, efficiently, and safely. With meditation, "good form" refers to the mechanics of breathing and the fundamentals of supportive posture. Finding a physically comfortable and stable position minimizes distraction and supports meditation. It's hard enough to focus under optimal circumstances, much less when your body suffers.

As you'll see in the following pages, there are some simple techniques that support good posture and engage your body in powerfully supporting your mind. This chapter also includes instructions for Mindful Breathing, a formal mindfulness practice that builds on the now-familiar elements of Mindful Breath and Pause. Mindful Breathing is a sophisticated technique that requires only a few minutes of daily practice. It also and simultaneously enriches your spontaneous application of Pause.

Following the instructions for Mindful Breathing while sitting in proper posture and some kind of regular routine provides physical and temporal support. It's hard enough to practice, much less to do so "free form" and on a constantly changing schedule. It's paradoxical, but true, that accepting discipline can foster the experience of a certain kind of freedom. The less energy you need to devote to the logistics of mindfulness practice, the more energy you can apply to the practice.

But be gentle with yourself. Mindfulness is for life; it won't always bring immediate gratification, but on balance, regular practice brings deep and lasting benefits. If you've ever struggled to stick with a daily exercise routine, or practiced a musical instrument, you know what I mean. Even when you *want* regular discipline, some days are simply going to be easier than others—no matter your skill and commitment. There will be moments of exhilaration, long hours when you want to give up, and even days when you do so. In the long run, you'll travel through all sorts of experiences and extremes. The goal is staying on course, moment by moment; it's not about reaching the end.

BODY AND BREATH

Both of the two mini-mindfulness techniques we discussed in the previous chapters emphasize focusing your mind on the action of taking a breath—without providing details regarding the mechanics of breathing. After all, you already know how to breathe; you do so spontaneously every minute of every day! The main task is to pay attention to a normally automatic action. However, neither technique explores the felt experience of breathing.

Most of us have almost no conscious awareness of the sensations associated breathing; we just do it. Perhaps you, like most people, tend to only notice your breath if you have trouble breathing due to illness, physical exertion, or nervousness. Breathing usually only draws our attention when it's difficult or abnormal.

In contrast, Mindful Breathing involves paying close attention to the physical experiences associated with inhaling and exhaling. To begin, let's focus on the sensation of the air flowing in and out of your lungs by following the progression below:

Phase 1: Feeling the Movement

- Place one hand on your sternum so your palm is flat, positioned centrally at the breast-line.
- Place the other hand at your belly (lower abdomen) so that the knuckle of your thumb actually rests in your navel.
- Breathe normally and notice any movement of your hands. Perhaps one hand moves up and down or fore and aft, or maybe both move. It's also possible that you'll notice hardly any movement at all. That's fine.

Phase 2: Noticing Where the Breath Goes

- Now take a deep breath, and see what happens with your hands. Do they both move, or just one? Is the movement primarily up and down, or fore and aft, or balanced?
- Take another deep breath and notice with greater detail.

Phase 3: Directing Your Breath at Will

- Breathe purposefully so that the hand at chest-level moves with the inhalation and exhalation, while the lower hand remains as stationary as possible. Take a few breaths isolating this movement.
- Switch the movement of your breath so that the hand at your belly moves and the upper hand remains relatively stationary. Become familiar with this sensation over the course of several breaths.

This progression distinguishes between belly breathing (which is marked by movement of the lower hand) and chest breathing (which is marked by movement of the upper hand). Of the two, belly breathing—also known as abdominal breathing—is physiologically more desirable. Belly breathing allows the diaphragm to drop so that the lungs can fully inflate and transfer air most efficiently. Ideally, a deep abdominal breath will leave your upper chest and shoulders relatively still.

Another, simpler way to prompt abdominal breathing is to position your hands horizontally across your belly so that the fingertips of your left hand lightly graze the corresponding fingertips of your right hand. As you inhale, notice whether your fingertips separate slightly. Then, as you exhale, observe whether they make gentle contact again. You might need to adjust your position to facilitate this particular movement. Once you become familiar with breathing to separate your fingertips, you can place your hands in this position to help you activate belly breathing at any time: standing, sitting, or even lying down.

Most people are used to the experience of chest breathing and even tend to take a "deep breath" by hyperinflating the upper portion of the lungs and causing their shoulders to rise toward their ears. This isn't the best approach. Vocalists, for example, rely on abdominal breathing, as do martial artists. Both disciplines benefit from greater breathing efficiency; vocalists and martial artists actually have to "train" with abdominal breathing in order to internalize the movement so that it becomes automatic.

As with any training, you are likely to encounter obstacles. For example, the tendency to "suck in" the belly frequently interferes with abdominal breathing. Many of us are (or at least try to be) aware of holding in our waistline, either for the sake of fashion or to develop core strength. But abdominal breathing doesn't mean that your belly will become soft or hang loose. In fact, moving the belly in and out actually exercises the abdominal muscles. As you become more skilled with isolating the movement, you'll feel how to maintain the muscle tone as you expand and contract your lower belly.

Furthermore, with practice, you'll also notice an added bonus associated with abdominal breathing: your posture will improve as your shoulders naturally relax and your chest broadens without being forced. This is especially noticeable when you assume a seated posture marked by a series of more or less ninety-degree angles.

Proper Posture

The easiest way to reach the correct posture is by scooting forward on your chair so that your feet are flat the ground and a comfortable width apart. Once in that position, follow the directions below:

- Check the position of your knees so that your lower legs are at a ninety-degree angle to your thighs, and your ankles join your feet to your lower legs at another ninety-degree angle. You might need to try different chairs or change the height of your seat to accommodate the length of your legs. Finding a chair that's the right height is the key to sitting comfortably and stably during meditation.
- Move your pelvis so that your thighs and torso form a ninety-degree angle at the hip. The idea is to have a slight concave curve in your lower back (your lumbar region). In this position, your spine will straighten and naturally support the weight of your upper body.
- Position your arms at the side of your torso so that your upper arms drop alongside of your ribs and your lower arms extend forward, enabling your hands to rest palm-down on your thighs. The following progression can help you achieve this position:

    1) Begin with your hands on your knees.
    2) Slowly slide your hands toward your hips, moving your elbows backward.
    3) Stop moving your hands when your elbows touch the side of your torso and your upper arms drop straight down from the shoulder.

    It's easy to position your hands too far forward on the thighs, but doing so angles your torso forward uncomfortably.

- Allow your head to balance on top of your spine. Try tucking your chin slightly in and down so that your lower jaw relaxes and the cervical spine at the back of your neck lengthens. This position naturally releases some of the tension in the jaw.
- Keep your eyes open, and either gaze straight ahead or slightly downward so that your eyelids relax and close slightly. Definitely make an effort to keep your eyes somewhat open when meditating so you're less likely to fall asleep or mentally wander off into daydreams.

I imagine that you might feel fairly awkward right now if you just adjusted your posture point-by-point while reading these directions. If so, relax and sit normally. Then, when you're ready to begin the mindfulness technique described in the next section, simply return to a comfortable approximation of this recommended position. Use the ninety-degree angles as a guide, but prioritize finding a comfortable, sustainable position that allows you to sit still and breath easily from your belly.

It's time to dispel the myth that meditation requires sitting in an uncomfortable position for long periods. There is simply no sense to trying to meditate when your body feels utterly miserable. Rather than help you concentrate on the practice, the pain is likely to distract you thoroughly. A little discomfort is normal, especially if you are not accustomed to sitting in an anatomically correct posture. This kind of minimal discomfort usually lessons with practice, and a few minutes of sitting with it is fine. But serious discomfort is unhealthy, and associating meditation with pain is certainly counterproductive.

While I've described the recommended posture for sitting in a conventional chair, there are plenty of other possible positions. You might prefer to sit in a traditional meditation pose on a cushion or even lie down. What's most important is finding a position that allows your spine to support your upper body, facilitates abdominal breathing, and does not put you to sleep (the most common problem with lying down). The idea is to put your body at ease so you can focus your attention on your mind.

MINDFUL BREATHING

You're now ready to meditate using a formal practice. From here, the steps are very simple and build on what you've already done.

If possible, face a blank wall or gaze slightly downward looking at a nondistracting surface: a monochromatic carpet, a blank wall, or an uncluttered tabletop. When you look out and down at a forty-five-degree angle, your eyes will naturally relax. Also keep in mind that it's best to begin meditation practice in a quiet and acceptably private space without much noise or visual stimulation. You might already have a perfect place for meditation, but if not, do the best you can with what you have. Keep in mind, however, that the most important environmental characteristic is safety—it's tremendously important to be in a safe space, physically and emotionally, when you begin meditating.

Now assume your version of the recommended posture (described above), read these directions, and take thirty seconds or a minute to practice **Mindful Breathing**. You'll recognize the progression from Pause, but this version is different because sitting in the proper posture heightens awareness of the physical sensations. Go ahead and try, now.

- **Focus** on the sensations of breathing normally (ideally just through your nose).
- **Observe** (notice if/when you lose focus on the sensations of breathing).
- **Refocus**, if needed.

Reflect on your experience. Did you focus on the physical sensations associated with breathing, including how the air moves through your nose, throat, and lungs, and how it's then released into the environment as you exhale? Is your nose clogged? Maybe you observed how your chest and belly moved (or not). Perhaps you became more aware of how deeply you breathe (or not) and at what pace. Simple and familiar though breathing is, there's actually a great deal going on.

Next, shift your emphasis to noticing the experience of purposefully focusing your attention, feeling sensations, and then recognizing if/

when you lose focus or stop observing so you can refocus. There is a subtle but distinct difference between focusing on feeling physical sensations (to examine them closely) and focusing on the experience of paying attention to them. Consider the following, more detailed version of the same technique, and repeat Mindful Breathing:

- **Focus on paying attention** to noticing the sensations of breathing.
- **Observe with awareness** (notice if/when you lose focus on paying attention to the sensations of breathing).
- **Refocus your attention**, if needed.

This time, what happened? Were you able to isolate the experience of focusing your attention and/or being aware of observing? Did you notice if/when you stopped focusing on the sensation of breathing? Perhaps you took a mental detour and began thinking about the sensations or judging them (as opposed to simply noticing them). Remember, developing the skill to pay attention to your mind's movement is your top priority. At this point, you might only be able to stay focused single-pointedly very briefly, but the duration of focus is actually less important than the act of *maintaining awareness* of keeping or losing your focus.

As a beginning meditator—and even as a more experienced meditator—your mind is going to wander off task. That's what the mind does; it moves. The practice of mindfulness meditation encompasses this movement through developing awareness of the movement. Noticing that you've lost focus means that you are developing mindfulness.

Once again, spend thirty seconds or a minute focusing and noticing what happens when you practice Mindful Breathing:

- **Focus.**
- **Observe.**
- **Refocus.**

By now, you've practiced Mindful Breathing for three brief sessions, which means you've already completed today's portion of the meditation routine suggested earlier. That's it. Of course, if you're enjoying the experience, you might add another session later or breathe mindfully for a little longer the next time. But be sure to end your meditation session while you still feel good about the experience. Its fine to stick with it while feeling bored or slightly uncomfortable for a brief period of time, but don't stick with it to the point where meditating becomes unpleasant. Instead, pace yourself so you enjoy the process of becoming familiar with the practice and develop confidence along the way.

MY WALL, YOUR WALL

I began thinking about pacing and making time for meditation almost immediately after I began practicing again in earnest and on my own. I hadn't thought about such things at the Zen monastery where a group of us meditated together, on a schedule and for a set period of time. In some ways, that was much easier—just as it's often easier to attend a regularly scheduled exercise class at the gym rather than fit in a solo workout at home.

After that first meditation class in Colorado, I committed to practicing daily for a month. So there I was, facing the wall, each day, because experimenting with my mind was as reasonable a proposition as any other I'd encountered. There was no other place to go, and nothing else had helped me feel more at ease in myself or more comfortable with my daily experience. But realizing that developing mindfulness could be good for me didn't make the practice of meditation all that much easier. This is what happened when I faced that wall:

- I realized that I'd better keep on sitting, breathing, watching the f-ing wall because something good might happen. And if not, at least I could rest for a few minutes before getting up to do more stuff.
- I started to notice the constant chatter in my mind, and I was shocked by the cacophony.

- I resigned myself to setting a timer (at first for a minute, then for five or ten) because I couldn't resist looking at the clock.
- I used every ounce of willpower to sit still even though I had aches, pains, and itches in places I didn't even know existed.
- I accepted that my legs and feet always fell asleep, and I handled the anxiety I felt about whether I was causing nerve damage— knowing full well that fifteen minutes wouldn't cause irreversible paralysis.
- I begin to get interested in meditation because sitting still, silently, became one of the most interesting and dynamic activities of my day, and it was all mine.

I still sit and face the wall on a regular basis. Some aspects of the experience have changed greatly, whereas others remain fairly consistent. My mind continues to move almost constantly, although I'm far more aware of the chatter and therefore less likely to get lost in the content. I also take myself much less seriously. My interest in meditation has increased over the years, and I appreciate the elegance and power of that inner reinforcement loop: interest increases motivation, motivation drives practice, and practice fuels interest. After all, few topics interest people more than the experience of their own mind, and I'm no exception.

What about you? If you feel like you've "hit a wall" (or see a wall looming on the horizon), it's time to redirect your momentum and take a little time to breathe and face the wall. Of course, I had to hit the wall repeatedly before changing my approach, and so might you. That's fine. Most of us only begin meditating seriously when we run out of other, sexier, options. Sitting and facing the wall isn't much fun, and it certainly doesn't offer distraction from whatever difficulties plague you. That's the whole point—distracting the mind simply postpones the inevitable confrontation with reality, whereas meditating brings your mental state into stark focus, front and center.

BREATHING FOR LIFE

By the time we reach adulthood, most of us have hit the wall at least once and understand that stress is bad for us—mentally and physically. We know this the same way that we know that there's a cost to eating unhealthily or engaging in any number of other risky behaviors; ultimately everyone pays up. Most of us wish to reduce, if not avoid, exposure to stress. However, transforming aspiration into actualization is complicated and often hard.

After all, we feel stress for real, and sometimes unavoidable, reasons. Furthermore, changing certain stressful circumstances can create even greater stress. If you hate your job but need the money, you're pretty much stuck until you can find alternative employment. Until then, you've got to manage as best you can and with as little collateral damage as possible. On the other hand, if your stress is caused by needing to care for a seriously ill or chronically incapacitated family member, there is no obvious alternative. Dealing with fixed external circumstances and situations that lie beyond your control is immensely stressful. Making and following a plan to manage stress is one of the very few constructive options available.

Practicing Mindful Breathing, three times each day, most days (or at least some days) during the week is such a plan. It's feasible for almost everyone; you can do it in private (for instance, in the bathroom) or in public (in the workplace). No one will know, except you—and you're the only person who really matters.

Following this plan brings benefits on three levels. First of all, you'll reap the physiological and mental benefits of meditating. Additionally, you'll also increase the sense of self-efficacy that comes with *taking control and doing something* to specifically deal with stress and challenges in your life. The third benefit is that you're making a long-term investment in your life. Literally.

Research now shows that higher perceived stress levels (among healthy people) are significantly associated with undesirable cellular changes. Too much stress can interfere with the longevity of your body's cells and your ability to make new cells. Chronological age progresses consistently for all of us, of course. However, the health of our cells can vary significantly according to individual characteristics and experience, including stress. In other words, stress makes you old before your time.

Premature cellular aging isn't the only risk associated with chronic or toxic stress. A study of US combat veterans from Afghanistan indicates that exposure to intense stress may heighten the likelihood of coronary heart disease among young adults. This finding is particularly important because the link between intense stress and heart disease emphasizes the inextricable connections between mind and body. Stress does begin in the mind (since the brain instigates the stress response), but the effects are utterly "real" in the body. And while we may not all face combat-related stress, the message is still relevant: intense stress leads to heartbreak, both literally and figuratively.

BE GENTLE

The research on stress is frightening, even if your life is not particularly stressful right now. Stress is such an intangible risk; unlike smoking, overeating, or excessive drinking, there's no particular external variable to identify and target for intervention. Stress sort of lurks in the shadows, and its approach is often so subtle and insidious that we fail to recognize just how stressed we really are—until we begin to experience more discrete problems. Maybe you get chronic headaches, or develop an ulcer, or perhaps your cardiac stress test sets off alarms. At that point, your doctor (or your spouse, best friend, or even your own inner voice) is likely to advise, "You've got to reduce your stress."

Oddly enough, a typical response to that particular, well-intentioned comment includes anger and fear. It's annoying when someone tells you that you're too stressed out, largely because the observation feels like a negative judgment. The implication is that a stronger or better person wouldn't be stressed out. It's also demoralizing, because most of us get stressed out when life is hard, even though we do our best to stay healthy. We'd prefer to avoid high stress experiences, naturally, but sometimes they're unavoidable: job loss, combat, divorce, death. "Of course I'm stressed," you might think, "what else would you expect?" And you're right, of course, because in that moment you are as you are and that's reality. But being right doesn't necessarily preclude moving toward healthier experience.

Of course, once we're stressed out, we're often *too stressed* to start a stress reduction program. Trying out mindfulness for the first time in the midst of a severe crisis simply might not make sense. Sure, taking a Mindful Breath or using Pause can provide some relief in the moment, but following the detailed instructions for Mindful Breathing might be too much. That's okay, because the practice of mindfulness is about knowing what's happening now—as well as what's feasible in the moment.

If you're not in crisis now, you're in a great position to begin a more rigorous regular practice. Ordinary conditions might not be entirely optimal, because few of us live totally uncomplicated stress-free lives. But ordinary conditions are normal, and more than sufficient. If you can start now, you will build your competence and increase your sense of confidence with the techniques and catch glimpses of how applying mindfulness during daily life improves your whole life experience.

Beginning now also means you'll start becoming more mentally and physically resilient. The more familiar you become with Mindful Breathing, the more likely you are to Pause spontaneously under duress. Likewise, regular practice builds greater stability and less reactivity, which means that familiar stress triggers begin to lose some of their power over your life.

Developing mindfulness is an incremental process—and a lifelong practice. As you embark on experimenting with Mindful Breathing several times a day, you're likely to notice fairly significant variations in your experience. There will be times when you relax happily into the rest afforded by facing the wall. Other times, you might feel intense frustration when you still *hit the wall* even though you've been practicing for a while. There will also be times when you postpone practicing due to any number of excuses ("it's boring, a waste of time, stupid, uncomfortable," etc.). You might (almost) talk yourself out of sticking with the practice at all. This is normal, and it's the mind's best effort at deflecting your attention to keep you at its mercy.

Don't worry about feeling resistant to meditation; it's expected. Just notice your experience and apply a little discipline. The idea is to honor whatever commitment you make to exploring mindfulness over a reasonable period of time. This is important because giving the practice a chance to work within you takes time; developing any skill (including mental skills) requires familiarity and repetition. The challenge is to sit and breathe, facing the wall, often enough to see what happens. If, after a reasonable time, you like what happens and begin to sense that practicing mindfulness changes how you live, then you'll continue.

4 • Thoughts in Mind

THERE'S A LOT going on in the mind. There are myriad thoughts, emotions, and sensations, which appear in an almost unremitting sequence. Even when asleep, we dream. Some of our mental activity is constructive and insightful. But there are also plenty of neutral—if not distracting or destructive—thoughts and feelings. They are the stuff of consciousness and life, but the mind is capable of more than manufacturing and reacting to words and sensations.

Awareness is also our birthright; it allows us to notice the machinations of the mind without automatically being carried away by the content of our thoughts. Awareness lets us recognize thoughts and feelings for what they are: dynamic, usually subjective, mental events triggered by the exchange of energy between brain cells—and not an absolute or automatically objective expression of reality.

This chapter presents two simple and very powerful mindfulness techniques that support training your mind to notice thoughts and distinguish between their meaning and their presence. Parsing the content of a thought from the awareness of the existence of the thought helps reduce suffering by shifting your perspective. There's a difference between telling yourself a story, such as "I'm a terrible person because I…" and believing that storyline. It's the difference between fiction and reality. Whereas fiction is often compelling and enticing, reality can seem stark and exposed. However, the notion that our thoughts define who we are is fiction. In reality, our thoughts simply come and go.

MINDFUL COUNTING

The foundational techniques of mindfulness we've discussed in the earlier chapters create mental conditions that support developing insight about what's actually going on in your mind. In other words, you recognize that your mind engages in thinking and that the action of thinking is different from the storyline of your thoughts. Mindful Breathing, for instance, helps discipline your thinking and deepen your awareness by evoking visceral experience—the physical sensation of breathing—rather than intellectual analysis, which is part of why it works so well as an introductory mindfulness technique.

However, there is another, equally relevant and effective, technique that introduces mindfulness by working with a specific sequence of thoughts as the object of attention: Mindful Counting. The directions are almost identical to Mindful Breathing, except in Mindful Counting you'll focus on counting breaths instead of physical sensations. More specifically, the idea is to place your attention on a complete cycle of one out-breath and one in-breath.

Although you can begin a cycle of complete breaths with an inhalation, it's preferable to start with an exhalation for several reasons. First of all, with this pattern, the pause in between complete breaths occurs when your lungs are full of air. This is more comfortable for you; holding your breath for a second when you've got plenty of air in your lungs is much easier than when they're empty. You can try both ways to experience the difference yourself.

Secondly, counting breaths using the exhalation-inhalation pattern requires a certain amount of conscious effort. Most people use the inhalation-exhalation pattern by default, maybe because we're all so accustomed to inhaling when someone tells us to "take a deep breath." So purposefully beginning the sequence on the out-breath requires effort and engages you in the act of paying attention. Learning is most effective in the challenge zone: somewhere between tasks that are too easy (and therefore boring) and too hard (which becomes frustrating and unconstructive). Remember that the brain is a muscle, and so what's true for physical training is likewise true for mental training—

and the optimal pulse rate for aerobic exercise is higher than resting but lower than straining.

With Mindful Counting, the task is to place your attention on counting full cycles of breaths from one to seven without distraction. While counting, you observe whether you maintain your focus on counting, have other thoughts while counting, or lose count entirely. If you get to your seventh cycle without having any other thoughts, you return to number one and start again. However, should you notice that you become distracted, it's time to go back to the beginning and start counting again from one. Common types of mental activity include thoughts (e.g., "How can something so simple be so challenging?"), emotions ("I feel frustrated"), and/or physical sensations ("My arm itches").

The directions for **Mindful Counting** will seem familiar:

- **Focus your attention** on counting full breaths (exhalation-inhalation) from one to seven.
- **Observe with awareness** to notice if/when you lose focus on your counting. (Losing your place while counting is the indicator that you've lost focus.)
- **Refocus your attention**, if needed, and begin again on one.

Before you begin, consider that you might be able to multitask during this technique by counting breaths and thinking about other things simultaneously. If you have this capacity, challenge yourself to discipline your mind and focus solely on counting. There's no prize for getting to your seventh breath, so don't sacrifice the quality of your attention. It's more important to follow the steps diligently and return to number one immediately as often as necessary than get to number seven while multitasking. The idea is to practice focusing on a single object of attention, rather that reinforce the act of splitting attention between different tasks.

The main goal is to develop the mental skill necessary for placing your attention *where you want it* and maintaining your focus without distraction until *you are ready to switch focus*. Mindful Counting, like Mindful Breathing, provides a context in which to notice what's happening in your mind. Counting provides a discrete mental task as the reference point for noticing the quality of your attention *breath by breath*. Whether you count from one to seven without distraction or you only get to number two before you notice your distraction and return to one is not terribly important at this stage. In contrast, it's tremendously important to recognize the quality of your attention wherever you are in the count.

Enough thinking about Mindful Counting; it's time to practice. As with Mindful Breathing, begin by taking thirty seconds or a minute to train with the technique. Work in a safe, quiet place and assume the recommended posture to reduce physical distractions. Experience the technique:

- **Focus your attention** on counting full breaths from one to seven.
- **Observe with awareness** to notice if/when you lose focus on your counting.
- **Refocus your attention**, if needed.

Then, reflect on your experience with Mindful Counting. Was it easier or more challenging than Mindful Breathing? Some people find counting much easier because they like the structured intellectual task. Other people prefer the nonverbal focus on physical sensation precisely because it is less structured and less cognitive. What about you?

Since you now know two basic mindfulness techniques, how you have a choice about which to work with now. If you're content with Mindful Breathing, stick with that for a few more days, and then switch to Mindful Counting. However, if you find counting breaths easier, continue your mindfulness practice with this technique. If possible, take thirty seconds three times a day for a few days to practice one technique, and then switch to the other technique. A few days later, switch back.

Both techniques train attention and heighten awareness. They are complementary, and training with one will facilitate the skill that you apply to the other. When you become familiar with both and feel ready to work with another technique, begin practicing Mindful Thinking, as introduced later in this chapter. But keep in mind that Mindful Breathing and Mindful Counting are foundational techniques. Although you learned Pause first, remember that all mini-mindfulness techniques originate in these more comprehensive techniques. Practicing them diligently will enhance your ability to apply Pause spontaneously. They also work equally well as stand-alone practices or as mental warm-ups that precede more advanced techniques. Which technique you use is totally up to you, and, in the long term, you'll come to trust your sense of what technique is best suited to your own life circumstances.

Mindful Counting incorporates a specific sequence of thoughts (counting from one to seven) and draws attention to other mental events. The experience of focusing on the counting—and then losing count—shows just how frequently thoughts arise despite the intention to stay focused on one particular mental task. What's even more disconcerting is the realization that the mind is a wild place: often undisciplined as well as willful.

You might even have the horrifying thought that your mind is getting more out of control once you begin practicing mindfulness. Almost all of us have this experience after the mindfulness honeymoon wears off. The initial phase of practice that comes just after you begin is often marked by a deep and welcome sense of relief. Learning the techniques is relaxing, and using them provides a respite from habitual mental busyness. However, repetition develops skill. The more you practice, the more sensitive you become to what's really happening in your mind. So you'll notice the habits of mental chaos more clearly and recognize the growth of your own mental clarity.

My first experiences with Mindful Breathing and Mindful Counting were humbling. Initially, I felt great. Then I had the uncomfortable sense that practicing mindfulness caused my thoughts to rev up rather than calm down. I assumed that less thinking or simply having less chaotic thought processes would mark progress—so I worried that I was regressing. Likewise, other disturbing ideas arose in my mind, including the question "Why am I wasting my time doing nothing?" I wanted to quit, so I could go "do something" more productive than breathe in particular ways. Honestly, I didn't like sitting still watching my breath. I was bored, frustrated, and uncertain. I figured there had to be some justification for rejecting mindfulness practice without feeling like I'd given up on myself.

So I went to my meditation teacher and confessed that I "thought" I was going nowhere if not backward. My teacher laughed gently at my assumptions and made an astounding point. He said, "You're not having more thoughts, you're just noticing what's been going on in your mind all along." He challenged me to think about my desire, or more honestly, my drive, to "do things" all the time. I began to realize that staying busy wasn't necessarily as productive as I'd thought. Maybe staying busy all the time kept me from noticing, or even let me avoid, what was really happening. What if staying busy is actually a kind of mental laziness? As a typical Western overachiever, I couldn't bear to think I was lazy, so that very radical thought sent me back to sitting still, breathing.

WHEN MY MIND WASN'T FUN

The chatter that goes on in my mind now, after many years of practicing mindfulness, is of a far different quality and quantity than earlier in my life. Today, there's a lot less happening—which is not to say my mind has gone blank or dull. Rather, I've learned how to rest more easily in between mental tasks. There are periods without much action, and those gaps permit me to recharge my mental energy so I can apply myself more powerfully when it's time to work hard. Even when my mind is full of activity, I am less frazzled because I know, absolutely and through experience, that my thoughts are transient and this too shall pass.

In contrast, when I was in my early twenties, I was gripped by my thoughts and emotions. Deeply depressed, my mind was like a blender, constantly whirring with unconstructive and painful ideas about myself, my relationships, everything. I believed that my identity ("I") was defined by what I thought, and what I thought was not pleasant or productive. That's the nature of depression: you get in a groove thinking and feeling badly about yourself and your world, and that groove gets deeper and deeper the longer it runs in your mind.

The anxiety that often comes with depression is likewise insidious. Anxious minds are not present—they are constantly elsewhere. This mental disconnect from present-moment experience is a form of self-torture. Why? Because there is relief in the current moment; what's happening now is already in process, so you know where you are and what you're facing.

Anxiety causes people to experience a shift in perception, away from actual present-moment experience and into the constructed landscape of the mind. Here, the worries just keep coming, replaying the mistakes of the past and fearing the future. You lose touch of the sensations associated with ease and well-being and cannot imagine any other reality than your current one. This is a terrible mental space to inhabit. You're caught in a loop in which unhealthy brain chemistry spawns unhealthy mental habits, and these habits, and resulting behaviors, reinforce the imbalance in the mind.

If you have ever experienced depression, you know what I mean. Some people are biologically vulnerable to experiencing depression, whereas others develop depression because of extreme stress or traumatic events, including the loss of a loved one. Regardless of cause, depression and anxiety are painful and almost always evoke the cyclic repetition of negative thoughts. These thoughts, in turn, amplify suffering.

But biology is not destiny, and neither are we totally at the mercy of life events. Temperament, supportive relationships, and early life experience all impact the development of resilience, or the ability to bounce back from difficulties.

The difference between feeling well and feeling depressed is both physical and psychological. Research shows that the brain of a person with depression is structurally and functionally different from the norm. As a result, everything feels different than in healthy times: your emotions are too dull or too intense, either you sleep too much or you spend your days exhausted (or both), there's no pleasure in normally joyous experiences, and eventually, you can't even imagine the possibility that life could be good. Depression is a sinking, deep hole and sliding into a deep depression leaves you stranded in the dark without a glimpse of brightness on the horizon. You forget that there is any other way to live and cannot understand how life can seem so easy for other people.

I remember feeling completely baffled and simultaneously angry when well-intentioned and not-depressed people advised me to exercise, or start a hobby, or just suck-it-up and decide to feel better. They had no clue, and I needed better advice. Talking with a therapist helped but in some ways only reinforced my misery through focus and analysis. I felt frustrated because I already knew I was depressed, and I knew what life events had contributed and how, but '"knowing" and "understanding" did not seem to increase my motivation to get out of bed in the morning.

So I went to see a Tibetan lama and explained my situation. Fortunately, the lama had spent enough time in the West to be familiar with depression—since apparently "depression" is not part of the Tibetan concept of psychology. He was fascinated by neuroscience and its insight into the relationship between the brain and the mind. He was also interested in the mechanism by which mindfulness practice helps break the cycle of negative thoughts that characterizes deep depression. He listened compassionately and seemed to understand, and I felt better immediately, albeit temporarily.

I knew that feeling validated was only a temporary solution and would not adequately relieve my depression. I was looking for a miracle or, barring that, a radical course to change my life for the better. I asked, "Should I go on a long retreat, or meditate at home all day, or become a vegetarian and do yoga, or do even more intensive talk therapy?" He just laughed, gently, but still with amusement. "You could, but none of that will do you much good right now. You need to go see a psychiatrist and get some medication." I was totally dumbstruck.

The lama continued chuckling and commented, "You Western-ers can be so strange. You think that you can 'think your way out of depression,' but your way of thinking is part of the problem. So you have to do two things: First, you have to let your brain heal so it can work correctly and support you in training your mind. Your mind needs your brain to function in a healthy way, so go to the doctor. Then, come back and meditate."

"But isn't it a cop-out to take the medication?" I countered. "I mean, don't I have to learn to overcome my depression myself?" Again, he patiently replied, "You *are* going to guide yourself out of depression. Who is going to the doctor other than you? Who is going to take the medication other than you?" That made me pause to think, but I was not yet completely convinced. His final comment shook me out of my indecision. "You live in a time and place where you can access expert help and effective medication to heal your body so you can *work with* your mind. What are you waiting for?" He was right, in so many ways.

He knew that mindfulness practice offers great benefits to people with clinical depression and anxiety, but it's not a panacea for every-one. With hindsight, I see that his logic penetrated the dullness of my mind and the strength of his compassion gave me the energy to go get the help I desperately needed. I now see that my paralysis and indeci-sion were rooted in my depression. I was stuck in that deep dark place, and there was no way for me to climb out on my own because I didn't even know the shape of my own prison.

If you are deeply depressed (as I was) or very anxious, your brain is working against you and reducing your capacity for paying atten-tion. Although training in mindfulness improves attention and helps organize the mind, it may not be enough to relieve deep depression. Furthermore, you may simply not have the mental energy to practice those mental strategies that would otherwise be effective. If so, receiv-ing appropriate medical treatment can turbo-charge your recovery from clinical depression.

As your brain heals, mindfulness practice can play an increasingly important role, including significantly lowering the risk of relapse. According to neuroscientist Richie Davidson in "Becoming Conscious:

The Science of Mindfulness," "When you see that you are separate from your thoughts or your emotions you have a whole palette of different ways to be in relation to those thoughts or emotions, and this can break the vicious cycle of depressive rumination. This capacity to separate shows itself in different areas of the brain." In other words, there are structural and functional changes in the brain that mark depression and also indicate the return to health.

In my case, as modern medicine helped my brain function normalize, I returned to the lama and began training in mindfulness. The techniques provided an alternative to my familiar cycling with negative emotions. Also, my investment in taking the time to practice helped me develop the discernment Davidson refers too.

So I breathed and attended to the sensations... and I got bored. I counted breaths, and I became frustrated with going back to one over and over again. I told the lama. He smiled in that patient, compassionate, and infuriating way, and said, "Good, keep going. Remember that when you are training your mind, boredom and frustration are obstacles to notice and face. You'll find a way around them." Time, and practice, improved my understanding.

FEELING IS NOT BEING

Thinking about boredom is actually quite interesting. Early in life we experience boredom as an almost environmental condition: a child is bored when there's nothing (or nothing interesting) to do. Later, as adults, boredom continues to appear as a miasma or cloud that settles on us. We feel bored the way we feel hunger, as a gnawing sense of emptiness and dissatisfaction. Boredom is uncomfortable, so we run toward the comforting distraction of media, technology, social chatter, or anything that allows us to stay busy. The mind is ravenous, but oddly, the mind rarely perceives its own activity as worthy of attention.

If you haven't already, try taking a few minutes to analyze your experience of boredom. Just stay still, and think about the experience. In fact, let yourself think about boredom long enough to get bored. If and when this happens, what types of thoughts mark the transition from curiosity to disinterest? How does your body feel? What's happening around you? How do you experience boredom, and do you become less bored when you contemplate these questions?

Consider that boredom is simply a concept; it is a thought that describes a state of mind and might even give rise to it. Maybe we feel bored so easily because we believe that boredom really exists as a condition. But boredom isn't a place we visit, or a thing we can hold or see. It's insubstantial. "Being bored" is an inner experience not an external reality.

The way we speak about boredom is actually instructive. If you say, "I am bored," you are literally defining your identity as boredom. But there is more to you than boredom. In contrast, the phrase "I feel bored right now" offers a description of present-moment experience rather than an indication of self-identity.

You might wonder if I'm making too much of words, but language organizes how we perceive and process experience. If you speak more than one language, you understand this intuitively. Different words communicate different meanings, and literal translations often fail to convey the richness of expression. Although words inform and convey thoughts, they are not the basis of personal experience and reality. Developing mindfulness of thoughts shows why.

MINDFUL THINKING

Although a thought seems to be a single mental event, it actually has two discrete components: (1) the fact of the thought's appearance or existence and (2) its content or storyline. Regardless of whether I make a simple observation or delve deeply into a complex analysis, each thought appears on the landscape of my mind and contains meaning. Usually, the content or storyline of a thought grabs our attention completely—so much so that we hardly acknowledge the implicit existence of the thought as an event.

Typically, we take the meaning of our thoughts very seriously and rarely question them. As a result, we suffer—and not only when we are depressed or anxious. You might be completely healthy and feel

fine when your boss gives you the responsibility for a critical and difficult task in a high-pressured work situation. This is the break you've
been hoping for, and you have the skill to succeed. But you also have
some very typical and very unproductive thoughts, beginning with "I
don't know if I'm ready to do this," followed immediately by "if I can't
succeed, then I'm going to fail and probably lose my job." Given the
specter of such dire outcomes, you might think, "I'd better ask the boss
to let someone else be in charge."

When a thought is rooted in self-doubt rather than actual competence, taking it seriously can sabotage your own growth and advance-
ment. If you really believe such thoughts, you are likely to fail at the
task or ask to be relieved from the limelight, even though you have
the ability to succeed. In this way, some thoughts quickly become
reality.

However, if you learn to see thoughts as thoughts (rather than
truths), you reduce the likelihood of coming under their power. So
when the boss outlines your new task, and you begin the thought
sequence described above, you would be more likely to differentiate
between the appearance of the thought (the instant you process "I
don't know if I can do this") and its meaning. Having some distance
from the thought's content means you won't automatically progress
to the next, even more destructive, thought ("I'm going to fail"). You
have the chance to register the thought *as a thought* and refocus on
the task at hand. If the thought's content is really important, you will
remember and address it later.

Of course, this example only makes sense when thoughts are incon-
sistent with objective reality. If you truly are not ready or able to take
on new responsibilities at work, then obviously you need to communicate your position and defer. In contrast, if you are ready and able
to stretch yourself, albeit lacking in confidence, then developing the
capacity to shift from thinking your thoughts to noticing them can
make a huge difference in your life's trajectory. Although this makes
sense, intellectually, it's difficult to apply in high-pressured real-life
situations unless you practice beforehand.

Begin by assuming the posture that you use when practicing Mindful Breathing and Mindful Counting. Then place your attention on watching what's happening in your mind. The idea is simply to notice when a thought appears in your mental space. In other words, your task is to identify the act of thinking (signified by the appearance of a thought) as soon as possible.

Keep in mind that thoughts are very diverse, which makes recognizing them challenging. Having and acknowledging physical sensations ("My back hurts, my nose itches…") describes one type of thought. Noticing environmental qualities ("The room is hot, cold, noisy, etc.") is another. Emotions are thoughts too, so when you "feel" something you're actually "thinking." Finally, there are infinite cognitive processes that range from spinning stories, to making observations, and/or analyzing situations ("I'm thinking about thinking, but thinking about thinking is still thinking…").

Once you notice that a thought appears, simply apply a mental label to the situation by silently saying, "Thinking." No matter the content, just describe the act of having the thought with "thinking." Every time you see a thought, touch it with your attention and return to watching your mental horizon. The action of acknowledging a thought's appearance with the silent label "thinking" emphasizes the action of thinking over the storyline of the thought. As this becomes more familiar, you can sort through thoughts more effectively and without automatically getting caught in their content. You can also discard even the silent verbal label.

These are the steps for **Mindful Thinking**:

- **Focus your attention** on noticing when a thought appears in your mind. You can do this by silently labeling the thought with "thinking" and then returning to watching for thoughts. Or you can do this wordlessly without the silent verbal label.
- **Observe with awareness** the degree to which you can place and sustain your attention on the sequence of noticing and labeling thoughts.
- **Refocus your attention**, if needed.

Take thirty seconds or a minute to practice this technique. Don't worry if your mind floods with thoughts, and all you seem to do is repeat "thinking" without a break. If that's the case, stay with the technique a little longer and watch whether your mind experiences any breaks of nonthought between the thoughts. Nonthought is alert, not dull. It's simply the experience of watching when there's nothing else catching your attention (and therefore nothing to think about). Nonthought makes little spaces between thoughts, much as the silk knots of an old-fashioned pearl necklace create distance between the beads. It's not empty of mental activity because your attention and awareness are actively engaged.

When you first practice this technique, you are likely to notice that you spend (almost) all your practice time repeating "thinking." The sequence could be something like "The room is hot—*thinking*— my breathing makes noise and I sound like a—*thinking*—I sure am thinking a lot—*thinking*—labeling my thoughts with thinking is still thinking—*thinking!*" Just as, initially, you might not get past your third cycle of breath in Mindful Counting before you become distracted and return to one, your first experiences with this technique might be marked by the rapid succession of your thoughts. Remember, the point is to know what's happening (thinking) as it's happening (when you're thinking); constantly repeating the word "thinking" indicates that you're doing just fine.

Training your mind to focus, strongly and solely, on a specific object (such as counting breaths or the presence of thoughts) strengthens your ability to place and sustain your attention on a target, and it reduces your vulnerability to being distracted by thoughts or dullness. Whereas the former is obviously desirable, the later may be even more critical. For many of us, initiating the act of concentration isn't so much a problem as noticing—rapidly and precisely—when we lose our focus. This skill is especially useful for those with attention deficit disorder. Military service members, law enforcement officers, medical professionals, and others tasked with maintaining focus on complicated activities, despite the tedium of long hours when nothing happens, also benefit a great deal.

FINAL THOUGHTS (FOR NOW)

The progression from identifying with your thoughts to observing them is life changing. This shift of awareness is simultaneously liberating and terrifying. Liberating, because moving more lightly and easily through life becomes possible. You simply can't and don't take your thoughts so seriously. Terrifying, intellectually and emotionally, because you're likely to wonder, "What am I, if not my thoughts?" Yet just as this question arises from the experience of meditation, so too does the answer—or if not an answer, then the confidence to live comfortably with the question.

This chapter focused on constructively working with thoughts. Mindful Counting utilizes paying attention to numbers as a background against which to recognize the presence of mental distractions. Repetition of Mindful Counting trains attention and awareness but also can foster feelings of boredom. However, as we explored midchapter, the concept and feelings of boredom are thoughts, and recognizing their true nature helps alleviate the discomfort of the experience.

Training your attention and awareness through this technique works simultaneously toward two different goals: (1) you'll improve your capacity to focus and observe, and (2) you stop seeing the thought only as its meaning. You'll learn a great deal about your mind from this mental practice. You'll also develop the ability to recognize thoughts as thoughts as well as conveyors of meaning. The more easily your mind notices the nature of its own activity, the less likely you are to accept the meaning of your thoughts automatically. As your skill develops, so too will your ability to choose which thoughts are constructive and worthy of attention.

Finally, with Mindful Thinking, we worked with a technique that focuses explicitly on watching and labeling the action of thinking in order to distinguish between the mental event (of thinking) and its content. Developing the skill of discerning between these two components creates the mental conditions for increasing conscious control over your own mental experience. It's empowering, and it can also be scary. But as you'll see in the next chapter, developing mindfulness of feelings supports and strengthens your experience of emotional balance.

5 · They're Just Emotions

MANY OF US live at the mercy of our emotions. Daily life provides all sorts of opportunities for them to rise up and take over our experience. Most of us perceive our emotions as essential to our identity; we believe that somehow they make us who we are. As a result, we feel entitled to our emotions, which gives rise to thoughts or comments such as "I have a right to feel angry" or "You always ignore my emotions."

But emotions, like feelings and thoughts, are insubstantial. They come and go. Just as I am more than my thoughts, so too am I more than my emotions and feelings. This is really good news, especially if your emotions cause you suffering and wreak some level of havoc in your life. I'm not saying that emotions are inherently bad, or that somehow we should aim to become emotionless—not at all. Instead, the idea is that life is much more comfortable and constructive when we experience emotions *as emotions* rather than live under their tyranny.

Understanding that emotions are simply mental events and that feelings are not facts is the intellectual foundation for bringing mindfulness to them. This application of mindfulness promotes greater balance, healthier relationships, and increasingly positive behavior. You won't become dull or lose your unique response to life. In fact, your feelings are likely to seem more intense and your emotions more vivid, but less threatening or extreme. As this happens, you'll become sensitive to their presence and consequently less likely to give them destructive power.

The last chapter introduced Mindful Thinking as a technique to train the mind to focus on noticing the presence of thoughts while developing awareness of the process of paying attention to those thoughts. For the purposes of that technique, the umbrella of "thinking" includes any and all mental events. However, in this chapter, you will learn about the differences between thoughts, feelings, and emotions. Practicing this chapter's technique, Mindful Feeling, will hone your ability to recognize them for what they are and build your confidence in what they aren't. This chapter is about learning and applying practical strategies—analytical and mindfulness-based—to increase ease and emotional balance and extend the associated benefits outward toward all areas of your life.

THOUGHTS, FEELINGS, AND EMOTIONS

Psychiatrists view emotions as the outward expression (also known as *affect*) of psychological feelings, and they assert that feelings are triggered by thoughts. That is, thoughts give rise to feelings, which are then telegraphed to the world by emotions. Thoughts and feelings are internal and private, while emotions are publicized by expression, speech, and gesture. But the line between private and public is deceptive, and most of us suffer because we think we can obscure our inner experience from outward recognition. However, separating our thoughts and feelings from our emotions can be difficult, and life can get very messy when we don't.

Before reading any further, search your memory and locate a recent experience during which you expressed a strong uncomfortable emotion such as anger, impatience, or jealousy. Now search for the feeling at the root of your emotion. Look even further, and identify the thought that triggered the feeling as well as the event or circumstances that gave rise to thoughts.

I'll give an example. I recently spoke angrily to another mother at my kids' school. I was annoyed with her because I thought she'd shown an insulting lack of communication with me regarding an activity for our kids. My expressed emotion was anger, my inner feeling was annoyance, my thought was that she was inconsiderate, and the event was that I'd spent the morning trying to get in touch with her when she'd turned off her cell phone.

As a result, I expressed my displeasure through angry words and felt even worse. She responded rudely and presumably felt equally uncomfortable and angry. Unfortunately, our kids will suffer most from this situation because we, their mothers, probably won't arrange any play dates in the future.

Return your attention to your own memory, and run the entire sequence forward:

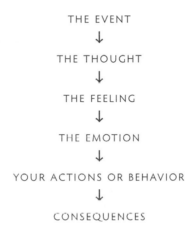

THE EVENT
↓
THE THOUGHT
↓
THE FEELING
↓
THE EMOTION
↓
YOUR ACTIONS OR BEHAVIOR
↓
CONSEQUENCES

It's much easier to notice the steps of this progression after the fact when you're not emotionally engaged and you have the benefit of hindsight. From this position, you might look back over the sequence and recognize how things might have developed differently. At any point between the initial event and the ultimate consequence, you could interrupt the chain or alter the outcomes.

Your frame of mind as you go through this progression, which informs your experience, is likewise under your control. Frames of mind are created by memories of past experiences and mental habits; they're not permanent fixtures of our identity. Therefore, having a different perspective at any given point also alters the sequence and outcome.

A friend described an experience that exemplified this point. She took her brand-new puppy to obedience school and found the other dog owners to be "competitive." She felt that the other dog owners constantly compared their dogs with hers—just as she'd experienced with previous dogs and previous schools. She felt angry and miserable. Later, my friend realized that it was her defensiveness that was actually making the current puppy-school experience unpleasant. This time, her puppy, the other people, and their puppies were just fine. Her assumptions, based on past patterns and memories, led to new suffering. Once recognized, those assumptions dissolved, and she could experience this round of puppy school afresh.

The consequences associated with most events are not foregone conclusions; they are the result of complicated progressions like the ones described above. Avoiding undesirable consequences—or achieving desirable ones—depends upon slowing the momentum that comes with emotional arousal and making mindful choices. Once the sequence picks up speed—no matter at which point—the progression snowballs. However, there are short-term and long-term strategies that can help mitigate, and ultimately prevent, the development of unconstructive emotions.

Applying Pause helps slow momentum so that the transitions from point to point are less heated. My experience with the other mother at my children's school could have developed very differently had I used Pause. Doing so at any point in the progression, if not repeatedly, would have applied the brakes and slowed down my emotional arousal and engagement. If I had noticed my anger rising, I might have simply canceled the plans earlier, thereby eliminating the waiting around that fueled my sense of aggravation. I might then have cooled down sufficiently for my conversation with her to be more constructive, and maybe our daughters could look forward to sharing another activity sometime soon.

Now apply the same analysis to your memory and replay the trigger event. Immediately insert a Pause before you start thinking about what happened next. Literally switch your attention from the event to taking one purposeful breath. Then bring your attention back to the event, and think about it. Pause again before—or as—your feelings engage. Then allow the feelings to come, and Pause again before you revisit the corresponding emotions shown by your outward expression of those feelings. Pause again prior to recalling your actions or behaviors, and Pause before you revisit the consequences of those actions or behaviors. Reflect on the experience of interjecting Pauses at the transition points. What happened?

You might have noticed that as you used Pause, the intensity of the memory decreased. Logically, that makes sense: by interrupting the flow of the memory you diluted it. But this experience of using Pause while working with a memory is predictive of applying Pause in real life, especially if you practice the technique when you are in less-charged situations.

You can even practice by picturing yourself using Pause in hypothetical situations, just as athletes and musicians mentally rehearse for the actual event. With adequate preparation, you can apply the technique automatically and appropriately when an event triggers a sequence that leads toward an unwelcome consequence.

KNOWING WHAT'S WHAT

The more you Pause in heated situations, the greater the likelihood that you *respond* rather than *react*—that you address a situation in a mindful and hopefully constructive manner.

The roots of a reasoned response lie in accurately observing the situation. This means knowing what's happening around you as well as within you—being self-aware enough to understand whether your inner experience is affecting the reliability of your external perceptions. Our inner experience creates lenses that tint our perception of external reality and may include past injuries that are not relevant to the present situation.

Physical conditions such as pain or sleep deprivation certainly skew the way we process and understand reality. Strong emotions likewise alter our vision. You might experience the same situation in radically different ways depending on whether you're floating on the cloud of new love or feeling really angry or frightened. For example, being stuck in traffic might make you roil with frustration if you're nervous about getting to a meeting or appointment, but the same situation might be a welcome break if you're stuck in the car but able to catch up with an old friend who is traveling with you.

In sum, accurately sensing your own inner reality is the first step toward accurately observing what's occurring around you. The next step is becoming more sensitive to how you process the information in your environment.

The human brain has the extraordinary capacity to process present-moment sensations very rapidly in relation to prior knowledge and experiences. So when you see something—anything—you notice its characteristics. Your brain then matches those specifications to memories. When the specifications match, you know "what" the thing is and probably access other information and feelings related to it. In contrast, you will have "no idea" what the thing is if your brain lacks any relevant prior experience or knowledge. When correct, this type of mental cross-referencing enables us to function efficiently.

However, there are real risks associated with incorrectly matching current-moment circumstances to past experience or knowledge. This can happen because your observations are inaccurate, such as when you misread the look on your spouse's face and respond with anger rather than patience. It can also happen when your emotions influence your behavior, such as when you hear your boss speaking in an angry tone while approaching you. It's easy to assume he's about to blame you for something if that's happened many times before. This presumption might lead you to react defensively, only to discover (to your dismay) that your boss actually came to thank you for something and wasn't angry with you at all. Projecting an emotion-based response onto someone or something frequently discredits—rather than distinguishes—us.

In some circumstances, the consequences are much more serious. Consider the following scenario:

In a combat zone, a soldier visually scans the surrounding buildings for potential threats while his unit sets up a roadblock. Earlier that week, a sniper shot at another unit involved in the same activity. As a result, everyone is especially nervous and under pressure. The soldier looks at a building across the street and something catches his eye: a movement behind a curtain in an open window on the third floor. Something pokes out between the curtains.

The soldier has to make a rapid assessment of the situation and take appropriate action. His unit could come under fire if the "thing" is a sniper with a rifle and the soldier fails to intervene by shooting the sniper first. But if he intervenes too fast and the "thing" isn't a sniper, he could injure or kill an unarmed civilian.

What does he do?

The outcome of this scenario depends on the accuracy of the soldier's situational awareness. He needs to know exactly what he sees in the window, and he needs to know whether his own brain processes that data with the benefit of prior experience but without prejudice. This means he needs to know whether his nervousness will work in his favor by increasing his concentration—or occlude his vision and processing. This information is critical as he analyzes the situation and determines the risks of various possible options. Finally, he needs to commit to a course of action (which might be inaction). Everything depends on accurate observation, and a life or many lives hang in the balance.

Soldiers are trained to develop situational awareness, but they often prioritize knowing what's happening around them and pay less attention to deepening self-awareness regarding the ways in which inner experience colors perception of reality. The movement behind the curtain could be a sniper getting ready to take a shot or a woman whose broomstick pokes out between the curtains while she cleans the floor. A soldier who has been repeatedly shot at recently might automatically assume that he's about to be shot at again, and he might experience intense fear and fire his own weapon. However, if he can monitor his own inner experience, he'll hold his fire just a few seconds longer in order to determine what's really happening. He and his unit will be safer because of that tiny delay during which the thinking part of his brain helps assess the situation and determine what comes next.

For civilians, this example might seem extreme, but it demonstrates our everyday response pattern. The risks associated with our observations, assessments, and actions may be less dire, but they're nevertheless very real. In terms of life and death, we also make split-second judgments based on what we see: for instance, while driving a car. We also risk relationships when we react with the momentum of anger or fear; we can break hearts when unfounded suspicion takes hold.

Likewise, we risk losing our children's trust when we make assumptions based on inaccurate observations, or past experience, and we shut them out when they need us to hold them close. Maybe your seventeen-year-old daughter comes home late at night (again), and you start chewing her out (again) as soon as she walks in the door, without even taking a close look at her face. Then you see her expression and realize that something horrible has happened. She's suffering and scared—and not because of you. Your patterned and angry response hurts like salt in her emotional wounds so she retreats to her room instead of asking for your strength, love, and protection. And your heart breaks a little too, because you lost a precious opportunity to soothe your child's distress.

Taking reasoned action depends on the clarity of our observations and the depth of our awareness, and "getting it right" matters immensely since actions inevitably send effects rippling into the future.

LOWEST THRESHOLD AND GREATEST IMPACT

In 2004, Matthieu Ricard, the world-famous biochemist turned Tibetan Buddhist monk and frequent interpreter for the Dalai Lama, altered the course of my career during a conversation on a very dark, rutted road in Northern India. We were both in Dharamsala to attend a Mind and Life Institute conference on neuroplasticity. Matthieu was an official participant, and I was a very grateful spectator. I was even more fortunate that I had occasion to speak with Matthieu, and the setting was symbolic—the rough road kept improving as we headed toward the bright lights of the town.

At that time, my work focused on exploring the role of contemplation in K–12 education. Along with others, I was looking for guidance about where, when, and how to target school-based programming. Some people favored teaching yoga, whereas others promoted teaching breathing to kids. Still others wanted to train teachers to model mindfulness in the classroom. I wanted to know what to prioritize, and especially what type of intervention would be simple to implement but yield the greatest impact. I asked Matthieu for his recommendation.

"Well," he replied, "you could teach kids how to be less reactive."

I was totally surprised by his answer. I'd expected something much more obviously related to meditation or attention training. Not that I thought he'd suggest that we teach kids to sit cross-legged and count their breaths, but maybe we could get their teachers to do that? Or, alternatively, implement curricula that would help kids train their attention and awareness using secular techniques rooted in traditional Buddhist practices. After all, the Tibetans have been involved in mind-training for thousands of years, and surely Matthieu could suggest some classical strategies to sharpen modern kids' focus.

My speechlessness must have communicated my confusion, because after a while Matthieu offered further explanation.

"Just think about the consequences when people make poor decisions and do or say things that aren't constructive. Today everything moves very fast, and being emotionally reactive can result in a lot of suffering. The consequences are rapid, and they ripple outward endlessly. So teach kids how to pause first and respond second. If you can do that, well, that would be wonderful."

The lights went on in my mind. Just as negative and destructive consequences self-perpetuate, so too would positive and constructive outcomes. By learning how to respond more and react less, kids could change the world. At the very least, the ripple effects of destructive energy associated with negative emotions wouldn't increase. At best, more responsiveness would increase empathy, compassion, and kindness, thereby creating the conditions for a vast array of desirable results. Best of all, the idea of reducing reactivity would make sense to kids; it's relevant and feasible, and the benefits are obvious almost immediately.

Older children, and especially adolescents, know that certain types of behavior typically bring them unpleasant outcomes; poor decisions can be clearly unproductive. But they often can't see the process that leads to their decision-making. Either they lack positive options, or they don't have the social and emotional skills necessary to make better choices. Habits can become entrenched simply because you repeat them. In addition, inertia at home and school makes it very hard for kids to explore, much less adopt, healthier patterns. A kid who gets into trouble frequently is likely to grow up with an identity informed by being in trouble (and being trouble). The stronger that identity becomes, the greater the individual's risks and resistance to positive change. It's as if the ripples from each destructive action flow outward like waves in a pool until they bounce off the edges and return toward their origin.

Matthieu's advice was to reduce the number of actions generating those negative ripples and, simultaneously, to reduce the impact when those waves bounced back. It was—and is—brilliant advice. The challenge lies in figuring out how to help people learn to respond more and react less. Fortunately, convincing people of the benefits associated with this course of action is fairly easy: most of us are acutely aware of the trouble we bring on ourselves when we react impulsively. But like the kids we once were, we still don't know how to function differently.

MINDFUL FEELING

During early chapters, you set the groundwork for training the skills that promote reasoned response over impulsive reaction. Mindful Breathing and Mindful Counting increase focus and hone awareness. With practice, and over time, these techniques will improve your ability to focus your attention on the object of your choice and sustain your focus as long as you wish. Once you gain some familiarity with the process of training attention and awareness, Mindful Thinking allows you to focus your attention on the movement of your mind and to recognize thoughts as insubstantial mental events. The next step is developing mindfulness of your feelings (in this case, emotional rather than physical). Witnessing feelings—how they arise, how they come and go—means you can work with them, and that means you can manage them rather than exist at their mercy.

This mindfulness technique involves placing your attention on your feelings, recognizing and labeling them without engaging in their content, and then returning your attention to watching for what comes next. This is a variation on Mindful Thinking; the steps are almost identical. With this technique, you watch for, and label, feelings. You allow other types of thoughts and even physical sensations to appear and disappear on their own, without acknowledgment. So if the thought "I wonder what time it is?" arises, simply disregard it, but say "feeling" to yourself if you notice that you *feel* anxious because you are running out of time or bored because this technique is taking too long.

Here are the simple steps for **Mindful Feeling, Part 1**:

- **Focus your attention** on watching when feelings appear in your mind, label them by silently stating "feeling," and return to noticing if/when feelings appear.
- **Observe with awareness** the degree to which you can place and sustain your attention on the sequence of noticing and labeling feelings.
- **Refocus your attention**, if needed.

Take thirty seconds or a minute to practice this technique. Reflect on the experience of scanning your mental activity for feelings and acknowledging them specifically. Feelings differ from thoughts and physical sensations because they evoke emotion. However, their behavior is the same: they come and go, arising in your mind and passing through your consciousness until they disappear. All feelings, regardless of content, share these characteristics—they're just feelings.

However, there are differences between positive and negative feelings—especially with regard to your treatment of them. With this technique, just as with Pause, we can learn to switch the focus of our attention away from negative feelings and curb or eliminate inner dialogue about the content of these feelings.

The next technique, Mindful Feeling, Part 2, helps us purposefully respond to feelings according to their content. In this version, you still scan for mental activity and watch for feelings to appear. But instead of labeling all feelings as "feeling," this time you notice whether each feeling is constructive or destructive. Simply sort the positive feelings from those that are negative. Acknowledge the constructive feelings with a sense of pleasure and return to watching. Alternatively, do not respond to the destructive feelings except by switching back to watching.

The idea is to reinforce the constructive feelings by paying attention to them and weaken the destructive feelings by ignoring them. In many ways, this approach is similar to actively rewarding children's positive actions rather than providing negative attention in response to inappropriate behavior. Eventually, kids tend to stop acting inappropriately when they realize that inappropriate behavior isn't effective. Thoughts are like children; they want your attention. Focusing attention on constructive thoughts, like appropriate behaviors, discourages undesirable activity.

Here are the steps for **Mindful Feeling, Part 2**:

- **Focus your attention** on watching when feelings appear in your mind, and notice whether they are constructive or destructive.
- **Observe with awareness**: if you notice constructive feelings, generate a sense of pleasure, and if you notice destructive feelings, do not engage.
- **Refocus your attention:** return to noticing if/when feelings appear.

After trying this technique, reflect on your experience. Although constructive and destructive feelings appear in the same way, your response differed according to their nature. You rewarded constructive feelings by cultivating a sense of pleasure, which encouraged further constructive feelings. Actively reinforcing the constructive feelings creates the mental conditions that give rise to other positive feelings. Ignoring negative feelings eventually reduces the strength and frequency of such feelings.

Feelings are catchy: not only do they lead to further generations of similar feelings, but they also trigger emotions that impact other people. Cultivating a sense of pleasure about constructive feelings tends to generate positive emotions (the expression of those feelings), which in turn prompt other people to feel good. Ignoring destructive feelings, and thereby lessening the appearance (and force) of destructive emotions, inhibits the transmission of negative emotional contagions. You know how this works: people feel happier in the presence of a happy person, whereas one individual's foul mood can infect everyone in the vicinity.

ACCENTUATING THE POSITIVE

Constructive, positive feelings and emotions make life easier, happier, and more satisfying because they increase compassion, kindness, and prosperity. Cultivating them leads to a better life: a life marked by healthy relationships and actions that leave the world better than you found it.

In contrast, destructive emotions increase suffering by strengthening anger, fear, greed, or jealousy. It's not that these kinds of emotions are "bad"; rather, they lead to behaviors that cause problems and pain for everyone involved.

Neutral thoughts exist in the middle of the constructive-destructive continuum. They're rarely memorable: for example, "I'm not hungry now" or "That car is blue." However, even these thoughts usually carry a tint of preference that results in a positive or negative bias. By itself, the absence of hunger is neutral, assuming you generally have access to sufficient food. But maybe you're not hungry because you finished a delicious and filling meal, in which case your contentment is positive. Alternately, you might not be hungry because you ate too much junk food and now feel bloated, or you had the stomach flu and lost your appetite. Similarly, perhaps you like blue cars and wish your car were blue, too. Or perhaps you already have a blue car, and you hate it (and by extension all other blue cars).

The point is that we have opinions, positive or negative, about almost everything we encounter, and these opinions impact our experience, for better or worse. On balance, it's easier and certainly more pleasant when the constructive thoughts and actions outweigh those that cause suffering and difficulty. Environmental factors can lead to this condition, such as when things go well and you have a "good" day. But relying on the external circumstances of your day to color your inner experience is chancy. We know that "life happens," but realizing that our thoughts, feelings, emotions, and behaviors are totally contingent on things beyond our control is profoundly uncomfortable.

In contrast, gaining some control over our inner experience offers the promise of greater stability and security. What if we could be okay inside even when nothing around us seems okay? This doesn't mean that we should be joyful or celebratory when we're in trouble or life deals us difficulties, but we can be *okay* with having to face the reality of those difficulties. While we cannot control everything that happens around us, we can control how we live within those circumstances. Perhaps happiness is overvalued or overemphasized in today's culture, whereas a state of peacefulness or normalcy might actually be a more realistic goal.

There are two obvious approaches to emphasizing constructive responses over destructive reactions. The first is deciding to "think positive"; this is a top-down approach in which you try to squash negative emotions while reframing everything more positively. Training our minds to see the glass as half full rather than half empty makes, superficially, good sense. We can learn to adopt a more positive perspective as we run into the typical obstacles and daily pains of ordinary life: getting stuck in traffic, or having to eat food we don't particularly like, or simply making the best of a bad situation. This works, at least to some extent.

But there are terrible things in life that, objectively and subjectively, present as empty. When a child dies, there's no way to spin the parents' loss in a productive, positive manner. Those parents have to grieve and feel the searing pain; doing so is expression and confirmation both of their love and their loss. But they can learn to notice the pain and come to live with it, rather than be consumed and likewise destroyed. Being mindful of their pain won't lessen the hurt, but it will help them survive it without triggering even greater suffering for themselves and others.

The problem with positive psychology is that it only offers a partial solution. Sure, you can accentuate the positive, but applying a negative strategy to negative mental events can't be effective. Deciding that "bad thoughts" are "bad" just makes things worse because you simply substitute one "bad" for another. It's like pruning a tenacious weed, where the more aggressively you cut it back the greater the number and reach of its new sprouts. In contrast, weakening the progression that leads to those thoughts results in fewer of them, and further reinforcement eventually makes the process irrelevant because the outcome is complete: if you don't generate destructive thoughts, you don't need to do anything about them.

This is the way cultivating mindfulness works as a bottom-up strategy. Instead of repressing "bad feelings" and reframing negatives as positive, you Pause and Pause and Pause again, interfering with the acceleration of destructive processes. By switching your attention out of the negative cycles, you weaken them at their core. It's the same mechanism by which withholding water from weeds ultimately causes them to wilt and die away, thereby making space for desirable plants to grow.

Have you ever been haunted by negative thoughts when serious romantic relationships ended? Maybe you replayed thoughts such as "I hate her," "He treated me like dirt," or "I'm never going to find someone who loves me," over and over again until they created a mental groove in your mind. Instead of becoming angry, disgusted, or frustrated with yourself because you keep thinking these thoughts, simply notice them and switch your attention to Pause, over and over again. Engaging the content of these thoughts is like fertilizing weeds; the byproduct of ruminating and wondering "Why am I torturing myself with these thoughts?" is that those thoughts become even stronger. Instead, you can weaken their frequency and potency by repeatedly switching your attention to something healthier.

Mindfulness also cultivates the mental conditions that give rise to constructive experiences. Training the mind to recognize thoughts, feelings, emotions, and behaviors for what they are parlays into improving your ability to pick and choose what you think, feel, express, and do as a result. Similar to the positive psychology approach, this involves purposely nourishing constructive experiences. However, the emphasis is different. Instead of positively reframing negative thoughts, reinforce those authentic mental events that are constructive. There's no spin with mindfulness; the idea is to notice present-moment experience as it is and skillfully work with your attention and awareness to entrain the positive while allowing negative thoughts to weaken.

With practice, the destructive mental events begin to lose their momentum and trigger fewer and fewer ripples of suffering. This happens by default, not by willfully deciding to cease negative thinking. With less reactivity, there is more mental energy for responsiveness. Then, as more constructive mental events occur, they create the habits that support similar experiences in the future. Thoughts, like some flowers, grow this way. Each mental event plants seeds, and constructive mental events carry the promise of greater beauty in the future.

As you can see, developing mindfulness is a process that takes you into new landscapes as you become increasingly skilled with the familiar terrain. You now know several techniques that apply mindfulness to breathing for mini-mindfulness breaks, and others that can form the basis for regular practice. Furthermore, you've used the three core steps of focus, observe, and refocus to experience thoughts and emotions more mindfully. You've learned that mindfulness joins mind and body in a rhythmic progression, alternately emphasizing paying attention to breathing and then using breathing to support developing awareness of the mind.

The next chapter goes beyond breathing and explores applying mindfulness to the full range of felt-sensations *in the body*. This broadening of awareness adds a new dimension to the experience of mindfulness.

6 • Being in Your Body

SO FAR, we've explored several mindful breathing techniques and other approaches that increase awareness of mental activities: thoughts, feelings, and their outer expression, emotions. In this chapter, we switch focus to experiencing physical sensations more mindfully. The idea is to pay attention to being *in your body*, not just to the mental activity or the isolated act of breathing, but to being present with the vast range of embodied experience.

We have five senses, and the information they provide contributes to the complex features of broader experience. Often we experience input from more than one sense at a time, and paying full attention to both simultaneously is difficult. Modern life requires us to multitask, and we certainly are capable of eating our dinner while watching television, but functional multitasking does not automatically correlate to having optimal, or even full, experience of any of your simultaneous activities. You might look down to cut your food and miss a scene, or you might not fully enjoy the flavor of your meal because you're focused on the dialogue. You were truly present with neither experience.

Of course, your degree of presence correlates to more variables than simply the number of senses you engage at any one time. After all, all five senses, if available, operate simultaneously even when you're not purposefully engaging them. Even deliberately focusing on any one particular sensation does not guarantee full experience. There are degrees of attention, and likewise, levels of awareness, and they are affected by multiple factors, including familiarity and priority.

New, unexpected, or particularly intense sensations usually catch our attention, but the ongoing, routine sensations more often go unnoticed. Just consider breathing, and the shift in your awareness of *how breathing feels* when you began Mindful Breathing. Those feelings were always present on the palate of sensation. The same principle applies to the ordinary sensations of waking, talking, eating, engaging in personal hygiene. So long as we engage in these activities normally, the sensations they foster simply aren't relevant or of high priority. However, their absence certainly catches our attention.

Many of us are strangers in the landscape of intense sensations. We rarely experience searing pain, exquisite exertion, or yes, the ecstasy of sex (for more on this topic, see chapter 7). It's as if we paint our lives in pastel colors, because we don't know how to work with the vibrancy of darker tones. Now, there's nothing wrong with pastels if you favor them over other colors. But missing the opportunity to experience greater intensity is a loss. Having the choice is what's critical, and that's where practicing mindfulness can expand your horizons.

This chapter applies mindfulness to the five senses: touch, taste, smell, hearing, and vision. The following pages introduce a range of practical and portable mindfulness techniques that isolate and engage the senses to enhance their vibrancy. We also examine the overwhelming experience of too much sensation and consider strategies to mitigate the stress that comes with being bombarded by too much stimulation. The common theme that ties these topics together is an emphasis on direct experience: the act of encountering fresh sensations as they arise, before engaging the mind in interpretation, judgment, or response.

MINDFUL LISTENING

The statement "I heard you" is simultaneously very simple and incredibly complex. At the superficial level, there's a subject (I), an object (you), an action (heard). The grammar is quite clear, but the meaning can be complicated and contextual. One interpretation is that "I" literally "heard you" coming into the room, or breathing beside me, or calling my name. Another interpretation implies a deeper subtext: "I" literally and figuratively "heard you" telling your side of the story, expressing an opinion, or reminding me of something. On this deeper, more complicated level, the mechanical act of "hearing" is intricately and rapidly entwined with memory, meaning, and analysis.

From an evolutionary perspective, it's a good thing that the brain makes the almost instantaneous leap from hearing a sound to understanding it. You can rapidly seek cover should you hear a pop and immediately associate the sound with a gunshot. In this case, the instant processing of raw sound can save your life. However, the equally instant processing of sound can also trigger reactions that put you, and others, in danger. It's easy to hear a particular sound, assume that it's a gunshot when, in fact, it isn't, and fire your own gun in response based on past experience and assumptions. Mindful Listening is important precisely because circumstances and the brain's reaction can move so quickly that failing to distinguish between the *experience of hearing* and *how you interpret and act on what you hear* puts us all at risk.

To begin, let's look at the three components involved with listening to your favorite music, for example.

1) The subject: you, or the person who is listening.
2) The object: the music, as well as the analysis and associations that you attach to it, such as "it's my favorite."
3) The pure action of listening: the mechanical process by which your ears process incoming sound waves and transmit raw data to your brain.

When you turn on your favorite music, your ears immediately begin transforming sound waves into electrical signals so your brain can process them. When the brain "reads" the patterns, it also makes connections with past experience, associations, and meaning. For example, you might hear a few notes from a song that give you deep pleasure as they immediately transport you into a distant memory of dancing on an oh-so-passionate evening many years ago. Sound is a powerful trigger.

When you hear a particular sound, your brain knows if you've heard that sound before and quickly indicates whether it's pleasant or not. If it is, the brain releases chemicals associated with pleasure, and you enjoy the experience. If the sound is threatening, your brain will automatically activate the fight-or-flight response. However, if you find the sound annoying but not dangerous (your neighbor's car alarm or the loud music from next door) you are likely to experience the stress of irritation. The rapid transition from hearing a sound to feeling annoyed about it demonstrates how easily, almost invisibly, the brain connects meanings and sound. Furthermore, the meaning we associate with certain sounds can influence our immediate actions as well as long-term behaviors.

Before learning about mindfulness, I simply never thought that the act of listening held any importance—except in the context of hearing something, of course. My ignorance caused me lots of confusion and misery. For example, I used to live in an apartment that was poorly constructed. Every day, I heard the sound of water moving through pipes embedded in the wall behind my bed. The first time I heard this sound, I felt annoyed. My annoyance then became a daily experience, and whenever the neighbor took a shower, I became angry. Of course, I knew that the sound wasn't the neighbor's fault, since taking showers is normal. The only obvious recourse was moving to a different apartment, but that wasn't feasible. So I was stuck, with the sound and my own response, and my quality of life suffered.

Eventually, I realized that my inability to control the movement of water in my walls oddly paralleled my lack of control over my feelings and emotions. I also realized that while I couldn't change the plumbing, I could work with my experience of interpreting and reacting to this particular sound pattern. This is an important lesson: there are a great many things in life that we cannot change, and trying to exert control over them is a kind of craziness that leaves us exhausted. Instead, it's far more efficient to focus energy on changing our own patterned reactions to minimize suffering. In this case, my task was to separate the sound of water from my own annoyance, and practicing Mindful Listening helped me develop the necessary skills.

You can produce the right type of sound for this technique with a metal chime or even by tapping a spoon gently on a glass. The idea is to create a very specific reverberating note that slowly tapers into silence. The progression of sound into silence looks like this:

VOLUME
OF SOUND

TIME

The basic steps for Mindful Listening are familiar: they involve the same progression as the other techniques we've explored so far. An important characteristic of Mindful Listening, however, is that you focus on listening as the sound diminishes into silence. The point is to emphasize the *listening* and not the sound; the sound simply guides your attention to experience *hearing*. Once you are familiar with focusing on listening you can use other sounds as anchors for mindfulness practice.

Training with the reverberating sound of the chime is beneficial because the sound is resonant yet simple. Begin by following the decreasing volume of the sound. Once the sound is no longer present, shift your attention to the experience of *listening* without anything specific to hear. The sound ends, but the act of bare listening remains. This direct experience of engaging the ears and brain to listen freshly, openly—without a particular object—is the essence of mindful listening

Here are the steps for practicing **Mindful Listening**. Begin by ringing the chime gently to initiate the practice.

- **Focus your attention** on the experience of listening as the sound of the chime softens into silence, and then listen to silence.
- **Observe with awareness** as you listen, and notice whether you stay focused on the experience of listening or whether you become distracted by thoughts about the sound, silence, or the act of listening.
- **Refocus your attention**, if needed (on the sound, or later, on the experience of listening to silence).

As you practice the technique, notice what happens to your attention, from the point at which you first hear the sound until the volume decreases, leaving silence to fill in the void. You might notice that identifying the sound helps focus your attention. Then, as you strain to hear the softening sound, you might become aware of the increasing sharpness of your attention. Finally, while listening to silence, you might notice how heightened attention merges with wide awareness. The idea is to focus precisely as you listen to the infinite silence.

Sound is like air: it fills space invisibly. We tend to notice when something fills the space rather than the openness, itself. It's much easier to focus on the object (in this case, the sound of the chime) than the verb (listening), especially when there isn't a distinctive object. Mindful Listening means becoming intimately familiar with the verb, so that you discover the object freshly in each instance. Obviously, you are the subject because you are listening, but with practice you are likely to notice that you pay more attention to the act of listening than to "who" is doing so, or "what" is heard.

TOUCH: MINDFULNESS OF STATIC SENSATION

Whereas listening to sound is ephemeral, the sensation of physical touch seems comparatively substantive. We can exist, healthfully, without the capacity to hear. But humans need to touch and be touched in order to thrive. More specifically, we need healthy touch, meaning that the contact is invited, developmentally appropriate, respectful, and when desired, affectionate. Just think about the importance of touch for newborns: babies cling to those who carry them, twine their tiny hands through hair, stroke skin, and even explore surfaces with their mouths.

As adults, the importance of touch pervades the mundane and the sublime. We shake hands in greeting or hug friends and family, and we pat fellow athletes to show support. We apply skin products (through touch) whose purpose, at least implicitly, is to encourage greater sensitivity to touch. And, of course, touch is the most powerful sensation in the physical act of making love.

Healthy touch is wonderful, whether you initiate and experience your own or share the experience with another person. Unhealthy touch is unwanted, uncomfortable, disrespectful, and potentially damaging. We teach kids to recognize the difference between "good" and "bad" touch, and encourage them to consider information such as "who" is touching them "where" and "when" and whether or not they feel uncomfortable. This is an example of how important it is to be able to observe our own physical sensations, inner feelings, and outer circumstances. So how can we practice these skills?

Right here and now, lightly place the tip of your tongue on the front of the roof of your mouth, at the point where the gum touches your front teeth. Allow your tongue to explore that region of your mouth. Feel textures and temperature with your tongue while also noticing how your gum senses the pressure, shape, and movement of your tongue. Now keep your tongue still and focus on the range of sensations present even when there is no movement to catch and hold your attention. At first, concentrate on the sensation in your gum, and then, the sensation of your tongue—first one, then the other—and then combine the data to form a comprehensive tactile picture that details your experience of touching your tongue to your gum.

Once your become familiar with the feelings associated with this particular placement of your tongue, you can practice mindfulness by using it as the object of your attention. Simply adapt the steps for Mindful Breathing by focusing your attention on the isolated sensations that arise when your tongue maintains light and steady contact with your gum. Here's how to practice **Mindfulness of Static Sensation:**

- **Focus** on the sensations you feel at the point of contact between your tongue and gum; breathe normally.
- **Observe:** notice if/when you lose focus on the sensations at the point of contact between tongue and gum.
- **Refocus**, if needed.

This particular technique is useful for several reasons. First, focusing your attention on a specific set of sensations at a localized position

in your body might be easier than paying attention to the more diffuse sensations associated with breathing. Also, whereas breathing is
dynamic, this technique involves a static position that is, by definition,
less complicated. As a side benefit, assuming this position causes your
jaw to relax naturally and without focused effort. This can help reduce
the strain and tension associated with clenching your jaw in response
to stress. Finally, even more than Mindful Breathing, this technique is
invisible. You can practice anywhere, anytime.

Mindfulness of Static Sensation offers a highly simplified alternative
to the widely used Body Scan technique, a guided meditation that
increases felt-awareness of the entire body. Although both techniques
deepen awareness of physical sensations, Mindfulness of Static Sensation works with a very specific, discrete point of contact in order
to avoid some of the potential problems associated with developing
full-body awareness.

For example, the effort to increase full-body awareness can trigger
deep memories associated with physical or sexual trauma. Body Scans
are powerful and can lead to constructive or destructive outcomes.
When implemented skillfully, especially by a therapist or clinician,
Body Scans can contribute powerfully to the healing process for sur-
vivors of abuse and assault. However, the experience of retrieving
or re-experiencing body memories can be surprising and potentially
damaging. For this reason, Body Scans are best used carefully and
with an experienced facilitator; Mindfulness of Static Sensation carries a much, much lower risk, and it's almost always fine to use on
your own.

MINDFUL MOVEMENT

Although stillness is helpful for training in mindfulness, making (or
finding) the time to be still can be challenging in daily life. The natural, necessary movements of life continue even when we purposefully try to stay still. After all, the only time we're totally still is when
we're dead.

Movement is relative, ranging from the nearly imperceptible motion of breathing in a deep sleep to the absolute movement of an athlete striving for ultimate performance. Regardless of intensity, mindfulness applies to movement. In fact, developing mindfulness of movement builds the capacity, even the habit, of moving mindfully. In the beginning, the emphasis is on paying attention to dynamic sensation to develop awareness of *how you experience* movement. As you become more familiar with mindfully experiencing movement, you can switch your emphasis so that you initiate movement mindfully. In other words, your perspective changes from paying attention in the midst of movement to informing your movement with mindfulness. This subtle but important difference marks the shift from focusing on the effects of movements (how it feels) to the act of moving itself.

There are many rich approaches that support mindful movement. Yoga and martial arts overtly address the skills involved with developing mindfulness. But just about any form of focused athletic or performing arts training will increase embodied attention and awareness. However, experiencing "the zone" while running, dancing, or swimming is not synonymous with purposefully training mindfulness in the midst of that activity. True, the zone feels like meditation: you feel present, equanimous, at ease in the midst of your effort. But in the zone, you *become aware* of paying attention to your present-moment experience as a result of physical activity. In contrast, with mindfulness practice, you *purposefully generate* awareness by paying attention to your mind. In essence, you feel present in the zone as a byproduct of physical exertion, whereas paying attention to present-moment experience is the purpose of mindfulness practice.

Distinguishing between the zone and mindfulness is important for clarification, not judgment. Experiencing the zone is wonderful. Developing mindfulness is likewise wonderful. Both are within the realm of human capacity, and they are complementary. If you know what the zone feels like, you're better prepared to recognize a sense of presence cued through mindfulness practice. Likewise, training in mindfulness will enhance your experience in the zone. By all means, aim for both types of experience. But consider that learning and practicing simple techniques to develop mindfulness of movement might be more immediately achievable than accessing the zone through peak athletic performance.

In fact, you can begin right now. Read the instructions below, and then practice **Stand with Attention, Part 1**:

- **Focus** on your breath as you rise from a sitting position to standing.
- **Observe** whether you inhale, exhale, or hold your breath.
- **Refocus**, as needed.

Repeat the process, as necessary, until you isolate the movement (or lack thereof) of your breath. Any pattern of breathing is fine, so long as you are able to move smoothly from a sitting position to standing. However, you're likely to find that inhaling is easier than the other options. If you didn't naturally do this, go ahead and purposefully take an in-breath as you stand up. You can visualize your lungs filling with air and lifting you upward, just as balloons rise when filled with helium.

The next part of this technique involves placing your attention on inhaling as you stand, and noticing whether you stay focused on the sensation of doing so.

Stand with Attention, Part 2:

- **Focus** on the sensation of inhaling while moving from sitting to a standing position.
- **Observe** whether you stay focused on your sensations throughout the motion.
- **Refocus**, as needed.

There are two main benefits associated with this practice. The first is that it's both discrete and discreet. The technique builds on your familiarity with mindful breathing to help you isolate one particular movement (rising to standing position). It offers a very specific motion as the object of your attention, and this, in turn, facilitates applying mindfulness to movement. The technique is also practical. Most of us can practice this technique every day, multiple times during the day. Even if your routine involves being on your feet for most of the day, you probably sit down to rest or eat and then afterward stand up. If your work is sedentary, you still have to move from sitting to standing throughout the day—to go to the bathroom or confer with a coworker—and you might even benefit from doing so more frequently. Furthermore, since standing up is normal, doing so with mindfulness won't draw special attention from those around you.

The second benefit is that this is another strategy for shifting your attention away from stressful dynamics in order to prevent or slow circumstances from escalating. Using Pause provides one approach. But sometimes Pause is too subtle an object of attention, whereas standing up mindfully is more significant. Also, if the stressful circumstances occur while you're sitting, standing up poises you to walk away and cool down, if that would be helpful. The next time stressful events start to snowball while you're sitting down, try Standing with Attention and see what happens.

Of course, there are stressful circumstances in which you are either already standing or not able to rise up out of your chair. At these times, you can try variations of the same technique. You might squeeze your toes hard, inside your shoes, until you notice that the squeezing becomes uncomfortable. At that point, relax your toes while focusing on the sensation. The basic idea is to shift your attention to a brief but intense physical motion in order to create a small break in the momentum of stressful situations. Another option is to purposefully squeeze a stress ball, or a wad of cloth, tightly in your hand and then allow your fingers to relax. Absent something to hold in your hand, it's better to squeeze your toes than your fingers because fingernails can draw blood. Also, no one else can see what happens inside your shoes.

MINDFULNESS AND SUBTLE TOUCH

Standing up, like squeezing your toes or fingers, involves one discrete and rather significant motion. But we also make much smaller movements, such as brushing our hair, shading our eyes from glare, or even pursing our lips. With practice we can also apply mindfulness to the most minimal of motions.

Learning Mindfulness of Dynamic Sensation is a good way to begin. Start by placing your right hand, palm down, on a supportive surface such as your thigh, a table, or even a pillow. Now lightly touch the tip of your left-hand index finger to the upper surface of your right hand. Slowly and gently move your index finger, exploring the top of your right hand from your wrist to the tips of your fingers. Take about thirty seconds to focus your attention on the sensations that come from this action, and notice the feelings registered by the skin on the top of your hand as well as at the end of your index finger. Here are the steps for **Mindfulness of Dynamic Sensation**:

- **Focus** on the sensations as you move your left index finger on top of your other hand.
- **Observe**: notice if/when you lose focus on the sensations at the point of contact between your finger and the other hand.
- **Refocus**, if needed.

Once you've tried this technique, consider that there are three possible ways that your brain will register this sensory experience. You might (1) feel the sensation at the tip of your finger more strongly than on the top of your hand; (2) feel the sensation on the top of your hand more strongly than at the tip of your finger; (3) feel both sensations more or less equally.

Reflect on how you initially registered these sensations. Then practice Mindfulness of Dynamic Sensation two more times, so that you can volitionally experience the other two options. The difference in experience among these three options is fundamentally about emphasis and parsing out the components. The idea is to differentiate among (1) passively sensing movement as registered by skin on top of your right hand; (2) actively sensing movement at the tip of your index finger; and (3) merging both access points of sensation to gain a two-sided experience.

TOO MUCH SENSATION

Increasing mindfulness simultaneously intensifies perception. You probably encountered this phenomenon earlier when you began practicing Mindful Breathing or Mindful Thinking. Usually, after the first few sessions, the mind seems busier or crazier than ever before. But in fact, the mind is just doing what it's always done—moving—and mindfulness accounts for the difference in perception. You're simply noticing your mind, albeit more clearly and more sensitively.

The same phenomenon applies with mindfulness of sensation. You might feel overwhelmed by the intensity of sensation that you've noticed by practicing the techniques described in this chapter. There are two reasons for this. The first is that you're simply paying much closer attention to the way your body feels. The second reason is the sheer quantity of stimulation that you are now processing simultaneously.

These two experiences are two sides of the same coin: the first emphasizes the detail and intensity, whereas the second encompasses breadth of experience. You start shining this coin when you practice mindfulness of sensation, and, as a result, your experience of sensory input changes. This can be positive, if not ecstatic (more on this in the next chapter). But rapid and dramatic magnification of the intensity of sensation can also be uncomfortable, if not overwhelming.

You might notice several sensations at the micro level when you practice Mindfulness of Dynamic Sensation. Your finger, or more likely the top of your right hand, might start itching or tingling. If so, notice the sensation and then take a break before trying again. You might need to slow your motion or increase the pressure slightly by gently but firmly pushing your finger down on top of your hand. Sometimes light touch is simply too activating, and firmer pressure reduces the intensity. You can adjust the techniques so they work for you and still maintain the basic framework of the practice.

At the macro level, you might begin to notice that you "take in" more tactile stimulation than previously. For instance, you might be more sensitive to textures or the fit of your clothing. Or you might feel bothered by wind, or conversely, relish the breeze more powerfully than before. You might also experience a convergence of other sensory stimuli. It's as if your world just took on the qualities of high-definition film. With mindfulness practice, everything becomes more intense, which poses a challenge in terms of your response.

Much of the time, simply shifting your attention with a Pause reduces the snowballing effect of too much sensory input. Then when you return to labeling "feeling," you can try to emphasize certain feelings over others, just as you did when you switched focus between the feelings received by your finger, the top of the other hand, or both combined. You can also determine whether there is a feasible strategy to reduce your sense of overload, such as changing your clothes or stepping out of the wind. If you can do something simple to decrease your stimulation, do it. If not, then the best available approach is to find ways to manage your present-moment experience.

That's where you can apply some of the other techniques that you learned earlier. For example, imagine that you walk into poison ivy and emerge twenty-four hours later with horrible, itchy blisters. Your skins crawls, and the lotions and medications help but cannot reverse your body's reaction. You are simply stuck in a horribly itchy shell, and there's no way out despite the very natural desire to jump out of your own skin. Somehow, you have to let time pass and your body heal—without scratching. Here are some suggestions:

- Focus on the sensation of itching, noticing as much as you can about its nature. Then shift your attention to distinguishing between your mind's ability to pay attention to itching and your body's experience. There's more to you than itching, and while realizing that you can witness your itching won't stop the discomfort, it will give you a little distance from it, and that helps you tolerate reality.
- Notice how your mind creates stories about your current experience, and understand the implications. Maybe you're berating yourself for walking into the poison ivy in the first place, but this is only helpful insofar as you want to prevent doing so again in the future. Regretting your actions won't change your

current circumstances. Or maybe you're silently engaging in a monologue about your discomfort, something like "I hate itching, I can't believe I'm so uncomfortable, I've never been this uncomfortable, I wonder when the itching will stop, why can't the medicine work better…." Such thoughts might offer a little distraction from the physical sensations, but they cause a different kind of suffering. The more your mind tells you that you are miserable, the greater your misery. Yes, you itch. But bare itching is much easier to manage than elaborated-upon itching. The idea is to keep your itching as simple as possible.

■ Switch your attention to other experiences. So when you can hardly bear the itching, or *have a thought* that you can hardly bear it, switch your attention to something unrelated to your current status. Physical discomfort, like mental discomfort, is self-referential: it's about "me" by definition. But when there's nothing to be done that can help "me" feel better directly, it's time to focus on other things that can give some constructive experience, if not pleasure. If you itch, surely others itch too. Wish them relief, just as you wish yourself greater comfort. Find some way to help someone else, with some part of your being that isn't directly affected by the poison ivy: use your mind, or share from your heart. This won't actively ameliorate your rash, but it will give you something beneficial that you can do despite it.

A SPECTRUM OF EXPERIENCE

Mindfulness provides a sharp lens through which to experience everything: your breath, your thoughts and feelings, and your sensations. As the next chapter on Mindful Sex explores, applying mindfulness makes pleasurable experiences more wonderful and unpleasant experiences likewise more vivid. Rather than living in black-white-and-gray tones, you move into a high-definition world of color. Life is more intense, and you might want to reject the less desirable experiences with as much motivation as when you seek what's desirable.

Taking steps to reduce the unpleasantness in life whenever possible is basic common sense. But sometimes undesirable experience is unavoidable or the cost of avoiding it is simply too high. At these times, all you can do is manage the best you can. Knowing what's happening, as accurately as possible, is an essential support for dealing effectively with whatever life brings. That means paying attention to what's actually happening, in and around you, right here and now. That's the practice of mindfulness, and the more familiar you become with the experience of mindfulness, the greater your ease—regardless of circumstances.

7 · Mindful Sex

MINDFUL SEX feels better than mindless sex. This isn't a moral judgment, simply a statement of fact. Sex between consenting adults who desire each other can be incredibly pleasurable—physically, emotionally, intellectually, and spiritually—and the enjoyment is heightened when the partners are truly present with, and for, each other. Of course, while infusing sex with mindfulness can be the elixir of love, generating the elixir takes courage, effort, and skill.

The subject of mindful sex is not typically taught in traditional mindfulness programs, for a great many reasons. The most obvious is that secular mindfulness techniques, such as those presented in this book, developed out of monastic traditions—and monastics are celibate, even if lay practitioners (like us) are not. Furthermore, there is valid concern about the very real possibility that "mindful sex teachers" might abuse their power and cause harm to their students. In contrast, practicing and applying mindfulness in the context of your own intimate relationship is safe. It's personal and completely in your control.

For some people, being truly present with sexual experience seems to come naturally; others might have to work at it. This predisposition might be genetic, but it's more likely to be due to the powerful effect of life experience. It's much easier to be present during sex if you've been fortunate and had the benefit of healthy circumstances that support presence. On the other hand, many of us are familiar with being unmindful during sex: because of intoxicants, when we are indifferent about a sexual partner, or unfortunately, as a way to survive sexual assault or abuse.

Regardless of your past experience, mindful sex involves being present with whatever is happening—in your body, mind, and heart—right now. For you, this might involve enhancing good sex. Or it might be a private supplement to a clinical healing process guided by a professional mental health clinician. Either way, it's your choice *if*, *when*, and *how* you bring mindfulness to sexual experience. This chapter simply provides suggestions about private and safe ways to explore mindful sex.

KNOWING WHERE YOU ARE

Sex and intimacy blend wonderfully, but not automatically or exclusively. Reciprocally sharing body, heart, and mind with another person is union. It's as close as we get, as adults, to merging with another being. The potential for expanded boundaries is what enables sexual intimacy to be transcendent; it also creates vulnerability that opens us to danger.

This potential is our birthright, and it remains possible even when lived experience clouds its presence. Applying mindfulness to sexual experience is one path to realizing our potential; however, be advised: following this path can illuminate beauty, and it can shine light into dark corners. Confronting the past is the key to experiencing the present with freshness and clarity, no matter what's happened before.

Many of us are all too familiar with the experience of *being there in the body, but not the mind*. There are three broad conditions that tend to foster this type of dissociated, unmindful experience:

- If you become intoxicated and your ability to make rational decisions is impaired.
- If you're forced to have sex with a person, in a place, at a time, or in a manner that you don't want.
- If you survived being forced to have sex with a person, in a place, at a time, or in a manner that you didn't want, and the coping skill of "checking out," which helped you survive, persists even when you want to have sex.

Of these, the first is, by itself, probably the least complicated. For example, if you were drunk and had sex with someone you trust, and if you generally like having sex—then the risks are fairly straightforward. If your impaired state caused you to skip using protection, you might have an unplanned pregnancy or get an infection. These are potentially serious, of course, but they're also risks you presumably understand and that are likely to be present during sober sex as well. Being intoxicated simply increases the risk.

However, the ramifications of surviving uninvited, unwanted, and/or violently inflicted sex are far more complicated. If these experiences are in your past, please seek professional and skilled assistance for your healing process. Be careful if you decide to begin applying mindfulness during sex, because focusing your attention and awareness on sexual experience might trigger memories of intense and damaging experiences. Should you feel ready to start, go slowly and gently, and begin by developing mindfulness of sensuality and shared romantic experiences. Then, if and when you feel safe, you can carefully explore increasingly intense and intimate sexual experiences. Keep in mind that your partner and you should be absolutely committed to *stopping whatever you're doing* if your mind goes elsewhere because you feel uncomfortable staying present.

Regardless of your past, it's important to remember that whatever happened previously cannot repeat precisely in the future. This is true for blissful experiences as well as memories of indifferent, and also damaging, events. The past frequently informs the present, but past events do not automatically predict future experience.

KNOWING WHAT'S HAPPENING

Sex is an experience of—and in—the body and can carry significant meaning. Positive, negative, or neutral acts of sexual intimacy impact us. While there is an important difference between being dissociated during sex because of intoxicants or trauma and spacing out because sex isn't compelling, special, or satisfying, the experience of "not being present" is of concern. I'm not saying that every sexual episode is—or should be—characterized by total focus on passion and sensual fire-works. Not at all. But it is realistic to be present during even the quick-est or sleepiest sex. And all sex should, at minimum, be pleasant and respectful.

The role of sex, and its importance in your life, is personal and con-textual. Intimacy and sex are not synonymous, and even intimacy is not a priority for everyone. Indeed, it is possible to have an intimate and fulfilling nonsexual romantic relationship. Regardless, the field of sex is a rich one for exploring mindfulness.

You may feel some disappointment with your sex life, especially given the emphasis on sex in modern culture. But where does this dis-appointment come from, and can you transform this kind of disap-pointment in the same manner as with other areas of your life?

Consider: is your sense of disappointment associated with normal physical and physiological changes (such as from aging) and therefore inherent in human existence in which all things change *and sex as well*?

Or is your measure of sexual satisfaction (or dissatisfaction) related to an application of arbitrarily created reference points that serve only to cause you suffering? Honeymoons, by definition, cannot last for-ever, as all things are impermanent. The key is noticing whether you judge present-moment experience according to "how things were" or "should be."

Regardless, being mindful during sex offers an effective strategy for enhancing your appreciation of the experience of sex, and it begins with knowing what's happening when it's happening. And the first step is deciding that you really want to know.

While sex normally varies by event and from person to person, look-ing deeper into your sexual experiences can help you identify whether there are patterns that seem to define your experiences. Paying atten-tion to your mental and physical state during sex is the first step. Con-sider the following questions in the context of your most recent sexual experiences:

- Do you talk about what you're doing or just do it?
- What does your body feel?

- What's happening in your mind?
- Do you notice the sensation of touch, or does overall arousal and excitement distract you?
- What does your partner communicate?
- Do you satisfy your partner?
- Does your partner satisfy you?
- Does time go slowly or too fast?
- How do both of you act and feel afterward?

Notice how you feel—in body and in mind—after considering your responses to the questions listed above. Now Pause (and Pause again if you wish). Next, return your attention to your present-moment experience.

These are intensely personal questions, and the answers can range from one extreme to the other. Additionally, analyzing and remembering sexual experiences is almost as intimate as having them. In some ways, your brain actually repeats past experiences in the act of recollection, for better or for worse. So, to a certain extent, you reinforce bad experiences every time you replay them. Likewise, you reinforce desirable patterns by revisiting them.

Each time you return to an idea, past experience, or skill, you run the mental program for that specific event. Furthermore, each time you run it, you increase your familiarity with it and that, in turn, influences how easily and quickly you will repeat it. This is why we practice mindfulness regularly, so that it becomes familiar and informs our lived experience. It's also why good sex tends to foster better sex, and dull sex becomes habitual.

GOOD SEX IS BETTER

Conventional understanding equates "good sex" with your own ability to experience and provide satisfaction. Physical pleasure is the most obvious measure of gratification, but emotional and spiritual fulfillment is an equal—if not greater—gauge of ultimate satisfaction. Perhaps you and your partner climax every time, or perhaps not. But is that the ultimate goal or measure of your experience? What do you (both) expect? What do you (both) desire?

Human bodies feel sensations and respond in biologically determined ways, so climaxing—while physically pleasurable—is not necessarily intimate. Inversely, sexual connection that does not result in climax can nonetheless be extraordinarily intimate. While it can be frustrating physically, a lack of climax is not an automatic disappointment. It all depends on what the partners bring to the experience, in terms of expectations, and whether they join energetically as well as physically.

Applying mindfulness during sex can enhance your experience more than you've ever imagined, but paying attention and deepening your awareness can also reveal unpleasant and previously unacknowledged truths about your desires and expectations—and about your partner. The question is, do you want to know, and what does knowing mean?

Next time you have sex, watch your mind from well before foreplay until a while after the obvious conclusion. Notice the sequence of thoughts, feelings, and physical sensations. Do they all align, and do they escalate together? Or does your body want fulfillment, while your mind remains elsewhere or actively fantasizes that you are elsewhere? Obviously, what you notice matters, profoundly, but at first just notice and see what happens. Even if you realize that you feel little or no connection with your partner, at least the act of realization re-establishes an intimate connection within yourself.

Watch what happens as the sexual encounter unfolds. Watch, listen, and feel, physically and emotionally, for indications about whether one or both of you are present. Are you "doing it" together or is one person "doing it" to the other? Are you and your partner in synch, are you following parallel but separate paths, or is one of you less engaged than the other?

Did one or both of you check out at some point, perhaps after climaxing? Maybe one of you wished the other would hurry up so you both could go to sleep? Did you just go through the motions, maybe hoping your partner wouldn't notice, because "you didn't expect to climax," and you made the choice to have sex out of generosity, or obligation, or despair? Then consider, is the choice to have sex out of obligation or despair *a choice at all?*

This question of equality has everything to do with sharing the focus of your attention and very little to do with the logistical act of physical stimulation. It doesn't matter who does what to whom. It does matter whether you're both there—fully present and consensually engaged. If you aren't, there's an imbalance, and you need to know.

Sometimes you only realize what happened after the fact, when the wave of physical arousal passes. If shared intimacy informs shared passion, the aftermath will likewise be shared. But shared passion that lacks intimacy often becomes obvious once the heat cools. If you were truly "one" during the act of intercourse, you will remain "unified" when your bodies separate. But if your bodies connected but not your minds and hearts, then there will be space afterward, as well as a possible sense of aloneness.

For some people, aspects of a relationship other than the sexual one may emerge as most rich. These include shared commitment to raising a family, providing companionship, and loyalty. Without a doubt, these are critically important factors to a partnership. The point is not to weigh the importance of sex versus all the other marks of a solid bond, but to consider that each of these factors may or may not be significant to you and your partner. Sex is relevant in the context of a marriage or other romantic relationship and is worth considering with care and mindfulness. If it's good it may provide a powerful and vibrant chemistry that bonds two people. If it's absent or problematic (and especially if it goes unexamined in the context of a relationship), the issue of sex may become be a wedge that creates tension and leads to fissures. Sex can be magnetic: it can pull people together or push them apart.

Sometimes people make love especially passionately toward the end of their relationship, or even after it "officially" ended, as a last-ditch effort to rekindle their love. The risk of breaking up can heighten the intensity of reconnection and reaffirm the relationship. If turbocharging the experience of sexual union provides energy for working on other issues, then it's clearly constructive. But it's not healthy to remain on a perpetual, albeit intense, relationship rollercoaster. Ultimately, you need to decide whether your partner and you are willing—and able—to remain *with* each other.

Staying present mindfully enhances the physical and emotional intensity of your connection and can profoundly strengthen the bonds between you. Remember that giving someone your full attention is a powerful expression of love. So too is being *present in your body* while you are with another body. If you're not present, mindfulness can help you recognize your experience. At that point, you can make choices.

Certainly there are a whole range of circumstances in which the presence or absence of sex or its relative "goodness" may not be anywhere near the most important factor in making a relationship thoroughly excellent—but if you are in such a relationship then both you and your partner should endeavor to make that choice with full knowledge. Doing so provides the psychological nourishment of understanding why you're doing what you're doing, and believing that it's right.

The intimacy of sexual intercourse begins with each partner's self-awareness. If you want to experience union with another person, you need to know yourself. This is potentially scary especially since modern life trains us to compartmentalize.

Reconnecting with your spouse or partner mindfully can nurture your relationship. Furthermore, sustaining your special connection provides comfort, energy, and affirmation when the rest of life is difficult to manage. Mindful sex can be one way to do this.

PAYING ATTENTION TO SEX

Sex and attention both improve with practice, but bringing mindfulness to sex offers a highly attractive type of training, compared to counting your breaths. However, developing familiarity with the basic techniques of mindfulness lays the foundation for mindful sex. Physical arousal is distracting, and deciding to be mindful during sex *without practicing mindfulness under less distracting conditions* would likely be frustrating and ineffective. So keep practicing the basic techniques introduced in earlier chapters, and then experiment with focusing on sex as the object of your attention.

What You Feel

Begin by being mindful of arousal. Notice when you feel the first tingles of arousal. Then watch as the process of sexual excitement unfolds. Pay special attention to what happens physically, mentally, and emotionally. These three components are complementarily aligned during healthy sex. In contrast, the absence of one or more component is cause for concern.

Physical changes manifest externally and internally. They are different for men and women, but both genders experience an increase of circulation and energy in the sexual organs. Typically, men and women become aroused at different rates: men amp up faster, whereas women have a more gradual acceleration. Regardless of pace, the dynamic experience of intensely pleasurable physical sensation provides a powerful object of attention.

Mental changes accompany physical arousal: if you want to have sex, you're likely to focus less and less on thinking, and more and more on feeling. Put simply, the focus of attention naturally shifts from mental activity to physical sensation. However, if you don't want to have sex (even if your body responds with physical arousal—because that's what bodies do when effectively stimulated), then your mental activity will become increasingly demanding. Listen to your thoughts, and take action.

Emotional changes are a subset of mental changes, but they deserve acknowledgment because they do not, necessarily, track together. For example, you might *think* that having sex is a bad idea (due to any number of concerns) but *experience emotional desire* (because you feel love, connection, and/or intimacy with your partner). Alternatively, you might *think* that having sex is the right choice (perhaps because you want to have closeness with your partner) but *feel* an absence of intimacy, or worse, a sense of dread or despair.

Conflict between passion and reason is complicated. When compounded with physical arousal, it becomes even more challenging. For instance, you might feel attracted to someone who you know is not good for you. No matter how you proceed, do the very best you can to stay safe emotionally and physically.

Also, prioritize staying fresh and open to the instant. Each episode of sexual engagement is unique, and remaining mindful of your present-moment experience allows you to be with it. There are so many things to notice about sexual experience—your own sensations, thoughts, and feelings; your partners'; your immediate environment; and this special moment in your life journey.

Practicing Mindful Sex

Applying mindfulness to sex is similar, in essence, to bringing mindfulness to any other experience. The techniques are basically the same. Just as Mindful Breathing increases your ability to pay attention to the specific sensations associated with breathing, Mindful Sex involves focusing on yet another set of sensations. Also, just as Mindful Thinking and Mindful Feeling build familiarity with focusing on mental activity, Mindful Sex involves noticing thoughts and feelings. All of these techniques involve focusing on a specific object of attention, observing whether you maintain your focus, and then refocusing as needed.

However, the progression of mindfulness techniques from Pause to Mindful Sex is increasingly complex and comprehensive; the instructions encompass more variables, and the application becomes more complicated and intense. Mindful Sex practice, as described below, is multifaceted. While the three familiar steps are inherently simple, the complexity and challenge comes from your ability to emphasize different objects of attention. To begin, pick one particular priority (such as sensation or watching your thoughts), and then, over time, explore other priorities singly or in combination.

These are the basic steps for **Mindful Sex**:

- **Focus** on a particular object of attention while engaging in sexual activity. Identify and pay attention to one or more of the following: physical sensation, mental activity, and emotional feelings as you engage in sexual activity.
- **Observe** whether you stay focused on your chosen object of attention or become distracted.
- **Refocus,** as needed.

Mindful Sex encompasses more potential objects of attention than any of the previously presented mindfulness techniques. This can seem overwhelming, but you already know that feelings—such as a sense of being overwhelmed—are simply feelings. So rather than become distracted by thinking "Mindful Sex is way too complicated," begin by picking a simple area of attention from the list below. Focusing on that one specific issue will help you gain confidence with applying mindfulness to sex. But consider, sex is powerful and multifaceted, so the potential for distraction is enormous. Go slowly, have patience, and above all, enjoy the process.

Areas of Attention during Mindful Sex

Comparisons. Stay where you are, without reference to other sexual experiences. Notice if you begin to compare your immediate experience with others, regardless of which are more desirable.

Comparison fragments your attention and awareness. It's so easy to think "This is nicer than last time" or "Last time was so much better than now." Such comparisons launch you into mental time travel between past and present and cause you to lose focus on the here and now. If your thoughts lead you to compare what's happening right now with anything else, *including your fantasies or ideals*, refocus on reality.

Expectations. Experience your current encounter as it unfolds, instant by instant, rather than fast-forwarding toward a desired end.

Although expectations function much like comparisons, they propel your mental time travel forward into the future. This means you worry about whether the present will take you toward your desired outcome. Expectations are insidious, especially when they are unrealistic or unattainable. They set us up for disappointment by shifting our perspective. When this happens, we can easily overlook the glory of *what is* by focusing on *what might be*. If you catch your mind measuring your actual experience against any reference point, refocus on your direct experience.

Performance. Enjoy being in the experience, however it develops.

Worrying about whether you'll be able to perform (achieve climax and/or satisfy your partner) frequently sabotages what would otherwise have been an eminently satisfying progression. This is true for men and women, although men tend to worry about the obvious indicators of sexual performance more than women. For everyone, ironically, focusing too much on climax can prevent you from attaining it.

So instead of focusing on a particular goal, prioritize enjoying the experience along the way. This strategy both deepens and prolongs pleasure, increasing the likelihood of peak experience through reducing the anxiety associated with expectations. If you notice that worries about performance are occupying your attention, refocus on your experience of sensations in the moment. Each instant of intimacy is precious, and climax—though the most intense—is only one among many exquisite sensations available for your experience.

Immediate gratification. Seek gratification in your immediate experience—what's happening moment by moment—instead of moving rapidly toward the promise of future gratification.

The rush of intense sexual experience is so compelling that we frequently move toward it as directly and rapidly as possible. Sometimes "a quickie" is just perfect. But when you have the time and energy, take detours along the way. Notice the subtly of sensation, so that the rise toward climax isn't a steady upward climb, but rather a series of intervals that lead to mini peaks, followed by mini rests, until you reach the summit. If you realize that you're rushing toward the climax, then move your attention to your current experience of pleasure.

Hot zones. Remain mindful of the human body's vast potential for sensitivity and increase your awareness of those areas that rarely get attention.

Because certain parts of the human body are especially sensitive and responsive to sexual stimulation, we tend to focus attention and activity on these hot zones. The most significant of these regions are directly associated with specific sexual behaviors. However, the rest of the body is also capable of exquisite sensation. Explore touch and texture, temperature and tone. Saying the most powerful sexual organ in the body is the brain may be trite but it's also true, and the brain encompasses a far greater range of sensual experience than particular body parts. If you notice that you're paying attention to limited body regions, expand your focus to encompass less traveled landscapes.

Stamina. Pay attention to your body and your mind during sex. Although energy impacts the level of sexual activity, it is not necessarily linked with the quality of your experience.

Sex requires an enormous amount of energy, and if you take your time with it, you're likely to get tired even if you don't want to. So long as you have normal sexual function (and if you don't, then go to the doctor to regain this capacity), there's no need to worry about your stamina. If you need to rest a little, do so with patience: you'll recover and reengage. This is particularly significant for men, since fatigue is often culturally associated with virility.

Remember that there are ebbs and flows to everything, and periods of rest should punctuate high-energy activity. "Down time" is no less precious than when you are on the way up; it's simply different. Use the rest periods for intimacy and sensuality; doing so will enhance passion and raw pleasure. If you notice that stamina is occupying your attention, shift back to the here-and-now and enjoy whichever experience is available.

VULNERABILITY: UNDERSTAND THAT SEXUAL UNION IS AN ACT OF MUTUAL SURRENDER.

This fact is potentially quite scary because humans typically like to be in control. Furthermore, allowing yourself to surrender—to your own body's sensations, your partner, and the shared experience—relies on deep trust. You have to trust yourself in order to permit your body (and mind) to guide your sexual arousal and satisfaction; this means accepting that your body might feel or desire things that surpass your prior conceptions. Likewise, trusting your partner involves engaging with someone as a willing equal.

You also have to trust your shared experience. Spontaneity occurs when you allow your experience to unfold without forcing specific actions or outcomes. You can't know exactly what's going to happen next, and neither does your partner, because the shared experience develops through you both. This can be intensely beautiful and liberating, and it can also produce anxiety. So much depends on whether you feel safe—emotionally, mentally, and physically—as well as whether you are able to stay present, mindful, as your encounter progresses.

Trust is important no matter the strength or longstanding nature of your relationship with a sexual partner. However, the type of trust and the risks of extending trust during sex can change according to context. Every situation is unique, but a few generalizations are worth considering. Three major areas of risk exist at the beginning of a sexual relationship:

1) *Physical risks*. Perhaps your partner ignores a limit you set or becomes violent; perhaps you incur an unintended pregnancy and/or sexually transmitted infection.
2) *Mental risks*. Is this a "smart" choice, according to your own criteria?
3) *Emotional risks*: hopes and concerns surrounding the future,

vulnerability, the possibility of getting hurt, and the potential for misunderstandings or emotional messiness.

Of these areas, the physical risks are most likely to diminish with time and familiarity. If you stay together long enough, you're likely to address contraception and disease prevention constructively. Likewise, experience together will allow you to make an informed judgment regarding the risk of sexual violence.

In contrast, mental and emotional risks remain, although they tend to morph. You might wonder whether the relationship "makes sense over time" or notice that the dynamics change. You might fear that your partner is losing interest or is unfaithful, or your heart and body might wander. The stakes get higher for staying in a relationship as you invest in shared experiences, such as having children or owning property. In addition, there is always the question as to whether you grow closer over time or drift further and further apart.

In the context of developing relationships, sex tends to intensify the other factors. Applying mindfulness to your sexual relationship can provide insight into the relationship as a whole, including your motivation to remain in it. If sex is good, then you might be more likely to work on other areas that require attention. If sex is blah or bad, your motivation to build the relationship might wane, or you might decide to accept a deficit in that particular area of life experience (or find satisfaction in other ways, healthy or destructive).

The intimacy of sex is volatile and can overpower rational judgment. Sometimes couples split up because they can't live together amicably, but they end up in bed again because their chemistry is so strong. Alternatively, some couples lose trust in one another's attraction or fidelity but build a shared life because other factors keep them together. The bottom line is that trust and sex are central in relationships, for better or for worse.

One of the biggest challenges involving trust in romantic relationships (or really, in any relations) involves our expectations. We tend to believe that trust is at least semi permanent; once earned or given, we trust until or unless something happens that cause us to break trust. As a strategy for living, this perspective is practical. At some level, we simply have to take a risk and assume that our trust is well placed and durable. However, trust is actually extended and confirmed—or retracted, or broken—moment by moment. We operate as if trust is solid, but we intuitively know that trust is ephemeral and requires consistent reinforcement.

Applying mindfulness to trust helps soften this realization. Paying attention to the present allows you to trust another person (or yourself) *in the current moment*. Also, accepting that trust exists instant by instant becomes less frightening as we see, through mindfulness practice, that all thoughts, feelings, and sensations are similarly changeable. Having the experience of trust, right here and now, is precious. Whether that trust lasts is, well, somewhat irrelevant. It might, and it might not. The best we can do is to extend trust carefully, nurture it continuously, and watch what happens.

Trust during sex is no different. You might initiate the experience feeling a complete sense of trust, only to watch as your trust fractures. Or you might start off with a shaky sense of trust and slowly strengthen the feeling over time. The main point here is that we have to find a threshold for having *enough trust* to allow us to enter into a sexual experience safely, and this involves knowing that we can conclude that experience safely if we so desire.

How do you know if you trust a partner sufficiently to warrant taking on the myriad risks of sex? At the most basic level, you can ask yourself whether you feel confident that you *could say STOP at any time, and your partner would honor your command*. This doesn't mean that your partner will automatically welcome your decision to stop, but it does mean that he or she will, despite feelings of disappointment and frustration. If that basic level of trust is absent, sex is very risky.

So long as your mind is clear (that is, you are not intoxicated), you will likely know how viable it would be to stop an encounter. Knowing that you can set limits and trust that your partner will accept your limits should bolster your confidence and help you decide whether you want to proceed based on other considerations. If stopping is not an option, then continue to look for ways to get out of the situation. If none exist, then do whatever is necessary to survive; afterward get help.

Trust appears when partners know that stopping is acceptable, and trust grows as partners share. First, you have to trust in your own ability to know what you want and communicate accordingly. This then extends to trusting your partner in the basic ways as described previously. The next level involves trusting your partner enough to feel comfortable with your own actions and responses. Additionally, your partner needs to trust *you* sufficiently to take initiative and fully experience desire. Sex is safe when both partners are able to stay present, trusting themselves, each other, and their ability to manage relevant situational and environmental risks. When sex is safe, in this way, you have the opportunity to experience sexuality fully.

How Do You Know?

The only thing we can truly know is what's happening, here and now, in and around us. Mindfulness largely determines the level of trust we experience, because it determines our capacity to accurately observe and assess present-moment experience. As you train your attention and deepen your awareness, you'll know more in every instant. You'll also become more likely to recognize when your understanding is obscured by preconceptions, context, or emotional feelings.

Clarity supports making constructive decisions about trust, and trust is essential for mindful sex. This type of trust isn't guaranteed by marriage or stated commitment. Instead, it's based on having the skills and the confidence to know your own mind and recognize reality as you see it. Mindful sex both relies on and enhances such trust; this, in turn, transfers into other areas of lived experience, including the aspects of human relationships that are not sexual. In the next chapter, we'll continue examining how mindfulness supports relationships. We'll also explore techniques that you can use to cultivate and share kindness.

8 · Mindfulness and Romantic Relationships

THE INSTRUCTIONS FOR Mindful Sex, as presented in chapter 7, provide an example of applied mindfulness. Integrating the familiar three steps (focus, observe, and refocus) into real life (as opposed to a practice session) marks a transition from the artificial and formal structure of basic mindfulness practices (such as Mindful Breathing) to informal, dynamic application of mindfulness during daily life.

Since Mindful Sex can only be practiced in a specific context, it may well be easier than applying mindfulness to the long-term patterns present in a marriage or in the magical arousal of new love. Romantic relationships are far more complicated and multifaceted than sex. Therefore, applying mindfulness to this larger landscape of experiences can trigger seismic changes: fusing stronger connections, realigning differences, and sometimes uncovering fissures that were already there.

This chapter explores several strategies to help you infuse your romantic relationship with greater mindfulness. Some applications are quite simple and offer clear ways to strengthen what you already have. However, mindfulness doesn't automatically confer a rosy glow; it allows you to see what's really there. As a result, greater mindfulness can also illuminate less desirable aspects of relationships. Nevertheless, mindfulness practice can still provide benefit; it can serve as mental and emotional ballast during stormy times.

BEFORE THE BEGINNING

Significant romantic relationships begin long before the first date; we build intimate involvement on the foundation of past memories and future expectations. Consider the first time you met your current, or previous, romantic partner. The other person was new to you, but did you see him or her freshly, or was your meeting already colored by prior assumptions? Perhaps you'd heard stories about him or her and had developed some preconceptions. Even if you meet unexpectedly, it's likely that your mind flashes through patterned assessment and analysis. You might think "She's not my type" or "He's too short" or "Her job is interesting."

Sometimes real life actually aligns with our initial conception. Often, however, it doesn't. This can be positive; when reality exceeds expectation, a positive response can arise and create attraction. "I thought he'd be awful, but actually he is wonderful!" When we're lucky, we're pleasantly surprised.

However, many of us have spent time picturing our meeting with "Mr. or Ms. Right": what he or she will be like, how the encounter will occur. Imagining a desirable future is seductive, but it's also risky. Daydreaming is distracting, and constructing idealized situations populated by perfect people frequently obscures the presence of real opportunities in front of us. There are so many stories in which people search high and low for their soul mate, only to realize that Mr. or Ms. Right had been there all along. Or they turn down multiple candidates because they're looking for "the one" when perhaps there are many "ones" with whom they might have found happiness.

Creating storylines in the mind can lead to disappointment when reality fails to measure up against unrealistic projections. For example, although fantasizing about Prince Charming is a favorite pastime of girls, holding on to the notion can easily distort a grown woman's expectations about finding a partner. There's no problem with fantasizing; it's exciting and allows us to explore our own desires and identify areas of concern. The risk comes when fantasy slowly and subtly replaces or distorts reality.

Other problems can occur when *what's expected* compares negatively with *what is*. Sometimes a sense of revulsion results: "Based on her description, I thought she'd be perfect for me, but then I met her and realized that we have absolutely nothing in common." In this case, your mind—and not the other person's personality or appearance—sets you up to have such a strong reaction. Whether or not you "click" with someone is just the reality of the interaction, but the degree to which you suffer as a result is mostly an issue of your mind.

Imagine that you meet someone with whom you have no expectation of beginning a romantic relationship—and none, in fact, develops. No big deal. However, now imagine that you had invested a great deal of energy in hoping that this person could be *the one* before you meet, only to realize that he or she isn't. Most of us would feel some level of disappointment, if not anger, at this undesirable outcome. So what's different? It's not the other person, because he or she is the same in either encounter.

The major variable is your perspective, which, fortunately, is under your control.

Of course, while minimizing expectations reduces disappointment, doing so might not be realistic or desirable. After all, it's a very normal human feeling to hope for *what might be*. So if you can't or don't want to refrain from developing expectations, remaining mindful can help you recognize them for what they are. Knowing that you have expectations makes it easier to handle whatever outcome develops from them. You might still experience disappointment, but you have a higher likelihood of remembering that disappointment—like expectation—involves thought and feeling. These too shall pass, because they are contextual and insubstantial. Just as your mind gave rise to suffering, so too can your mind allow the suffering to diminish and disappear.

The main point here is that new relationships emerge in relation to existing expectations and past experiences. This explains why so many people have successive relationships that seem to repeat the same patterns, albeit with different partners. The people may differ, but the outcomes are likely to stay consistent—unless we pay attention to the underlying issues and stay present, so that the current relationship can have a life of its own. Although doing so can be often challenging, applying mindfulness *before* the relationship can allow a fresh encounter to begin.

A Honeymoon That Doesn't End

Mindfulness practice helps couples extend the freshness and passion of a honeymoon far beyond the conventional period of days, weeks, or months in two main ways. First, mindfulness increases each individual's capacity to remain attentive and aware of the other and their evolving relationship. Second, mindfulness improves resilience, helping extend the halcyon days of new relationships when the energy of discovery masks vulnerability. Couples need to weather the natural ups and downs of a new relationship in order to have any honeymoon period at all, much less an ongoing experience of wonder and union.

In the past, the designated period of the honeymoon gave newlyweds a dedicated time period in which to develop the physical and emotional intimacy alluded to in their wedding vows. The idea was to take a trip and physically move beyond the normal routine of each individual's daily life in order to create new, shared routines as a couple, including initiating sex. The honeymoon gave newlyweds a chance to enjoy each other freely and forge a unique shared identity before returning to their responsibilities. While the time period of an actual honeymoon is limited, the wonder and passion experienced during a honeymoon need not wane. But keeping them alive requires attention and awareness in the midst of the pressures and distractions of regular life.

Today, few couples fully experience old-fashioned honeymoons. Although many newlyweds take a honeymoon trip, most have already initiated sexual intimacy and/or already spent extended periods of time together. As a result, they have two somewhat diluted honeymoon periods. The first occurs when they first fall in love and bond through discovering each other sexually. The second is when they take an official honeymoon trip during which they might explore new geographical locations but have already become familiar with each other's bodies. Whereas many couples have spectacular honeymoons, fondly remembering that specific time period for the rest of their lives, others mourn, having realized that their honeymoon failed to live up to expectations.

From my perspective, any honeymoon is a gift, whether it's the honeymoon-like period at the beginning of a relationship or an actual honeymoon trip that celebrates your commitment to your loved one. Trips are wonderful, but having a honeymoon at home is equally as precious so long as you make and maintain boundaries that protect your space together. Take your time, and enjoy. Don't rush anything, just move at the pace that feels comfortable and is affordable. Stay present.

There's a magical giddiness that comes with falling in love, or falling more deeply into love, and there's no conflict between fully experiencing that magic and staying present. In fact, practicing mindfulness is likely to make your experience even more vivid. Just as mindfulness can make sex hotter and more satisfying, mindfulness likewise enhances the freshness and wonder of new relationships. In addition, being mindful of what makes your honeymoon period special increases your ongoing ability to sustain the essential qualities into the future.

People say that honeymoons end when the daily grind eclipses having special time together. Literally, this might be the end of vacation as you return to work and chores. But figuratively, it encompasses the transition between the first blush of love and the dawning realization that your partner (like you) has flaws and frustrations. This is the point at which love deepens for the long haul, and you trust that its strength will bind you together despite challenges. But just because you settle into a routine doesn't mean you have to kiss goodbye the freshness of honeymoon-like interactions. Here are some ways you can bring mindfulness into your relationship and continue enjoying staying present as it develops.

- **Focus on your partner; the gift of attention is a powerful expression of love.** All of us want to be seen—and cherished—for who we are. Make time to be with each other without distractions (including the kids) or expectations of having sex (you might, but you might not). Just *be* together, and see what happens.

▪ **Foster variety in your shared daily routine.** It's so easy to fall into the daily grind, only to realize that your days run together indistinctly. Try to notice if you fall into monotonous patterns such as coming home, having a beer, making dinner, hanging out with the kids, putting them to bed, watching TV, and falling asleep on the couch. You can still keep the essential aspects of a normal routine, but introduce little changes. For example, if you always eat dinner at the dining room table, have a picnic one evening on your living room floor. Mindfulness here is about recognizing patterns and infusing repetitive actions with cues to support fresh experience.

▪ **Notice if you use the kids as an excuse to avoid intimacy with your partner.** If your closeness with the kids creates distance in your marriage, notice it and reflect on the implications. You owe it to yourself—and your kids—to be honest and model a healthy relationship. If the marriage is unhappy, the kids won't have good role models to help them find happier relationships.

▪ **Find new activities and experiences to share with your partner.** Simple things are just fine, such as playing board games, sharing a new project, or walking in an unfamiliar neighborhood together. Creating shared experiences doesn't need to be expensive or time consuming. The idea is to generate shared memories of ordinary life together: not just memories of the spectacular moments (like your honeymoon), but ongoing collections of mental snapshots that you can likewise treasure.

▪ **Keep a diary of high points in your relationship.** There's no need for any particular schedule, but it is important to *make this record together*. This is not an obligation but rather a ritual that allows you to witness your present-moment experience by writing and reflecting on it. It will also help you remember the richness of your life together by creating a narrative. Draw pictures, paste in mementos, use your computer to create an album with text and music, or use any other medium you like. Remember, though, that the point is not to develop memories for the future, but to reinforce your present-moment experience; this in turn will enrich your life to come.

SHARING KINDNESS

Kindness is an elixir that fortifies relationships; it is the expression of an individual's desire that others experience contentment and joy. Kindness also replenishes itself when tapped. The kinder you are to others, the more kindness you're likely to experience within yourself— toward yourself—because the act of giving extends the gift to everyone involved.

All the world's major wisdom and ethical traditions view kindness as a virtue and encourage us to cultivate and share kindness for our own benefit as well as others'. And although people frequently think of kindness as a personality trait, in fact, kindness can be practiced and learned just like mindfulness.

Begin by reflecting on your own experience of kindness. How do you feel when someone is kind to you? How do you feel when you're kind to another person? What is the essence of kindness? Perhaps you notice an expansive feeling of generosity, because kindness is inherently a gift of goodness. You might also notice that kindness is soft and carries the warmth of caring. Kindness can lead you to smile.

Sharing Kindness is a mindfulness technique that uses the experience and extension of kindness as the object of attention. The steps should be familiar by now, but the emphasis is different. Unlike the all the other mindfulness techniques you've practiced so far, Sharing Kindness applies mindfulness to cultivating a mental event that carries meaning.

In the beginning, imagine a person toward whom you naturally feel kindness. This person might be a partner or spouse, child, parent, or friend. The idea is to orient your expression of kindness outward toward that particular person, whom we will refer to as "X." Read the following directions, and then take thirty seconds to practice **Sharing Kindness** toward others.

- **Focus your attention** on experiencing kindness and extending kindness from your heart toward X.
- **Observe with awareness** whether you stay focused on experiencing and extending kindness to X or whether you become distracted.
- **Refocus your attention**, if needed.

It's easiest to begin training in Sharing Kindness by focusing on another person for whom you naturally feel kindness. However, we can only really give kindness to others if we also know the experience of receiving kindness. Therefore, now that you've begun using this technique as described above, you might experiment with shifting your focus from that other person and direct it inward toward yourself. Here are the directions for practicing **Sharing Kindness Toward Yourself**:

- **Focus your attention** on experiencing kindness and extending kindness to yourself.
- **Observe with awareness** whether you stay focused on experiencing and extending kindness to yourself or whether you become distracted.
- **Refocus your attention**, if needed.

Notice which iteration of Sharing Kindness feels most attractive to you now. There's no set order for practicing, and both versions serve equally well as an introductory technique. Pick one, and then practice it three times a day, for thirty seconds or a minute, most days in the week. If you focus on another person, stick with that particular person for a few days, and then try switching to someone else.

Kindness helps all relationships, no matter their state of being. If your marriage is good, cultivating mindfulness will make it better: desiring that your loved one is happy is natural and reciprocal. If your marriage is rocky, purposefully generating and sharing kindness might save it. Finally, if the marriage is ending, kindness can help mitigate suffering for all involved.

MINDFULNESS AND CONFLICT

The absence of kindness fuels conflict in the world, in relationships, and in ourselves.

Conflict exists on a continuum of intensity and importance. Overt conflicts involve differences among people, from mild disagreements to violent engagement. Inner conflicts typically pit your conscience against your desire.

Conflict is common among individuals involved in significant relationships, and it isn't necessarily bad. Some disagreements are catalysts for positive change and can lead to new and better strategies for communication and collaboration. Even the most unpleasant disagreements still provide an opportunity for those involved to develop and apply conflict-resolution skills, which is important for everyone. Children, in particular, need to learn these skills; if they don't, and they grow into adults who are unable to use or model them, conflicts can ravage communities.

So what goes wrong? And why are some conflicts easy to diffuse whereas others spread like wildfire? In fact, this very cliché provides insight into the nature of conflict and its root cause: anger. The first stirrings of anger are like sparks: they flash in response to a trigger, and they quickly fizzle out unless they land on flammable material. Given fuel, sparks burst into flames that continue burning until the fuel is exhausted. Whether or not someone actively fans the flames, they will spread, consuming matter until there's nothing left to burn. Such is the nature of fire.

Conflict is fueled by angry thoughts, speech, or actions. Once raging, anger takes on a force of its own and seeks to consume everything it touches. Once stoked, the furnace of anger can explode into violent conflict and war, bringing immeasurable damage to living beings and the earth. This is the nature of anger, and its heat burns us in so many ways.

A marriage (or other long-term partnership) can encompass a full range of conflicts.

One end of the continuum encompasses minor disagreements that can easily be resolved, lead to greater trust and intimacy between you and your partner, and give you a valuable opportunity to practice your conflict-resolution skills. Of course, I'm not saying you should manufacture conflicts in order to practice resolving them, but there's no reason to view little disagreements with fear or judgment. Should such conflicts arise, remain mindful so you can learn through them. This is even more important if you have children; you can model healthy conflict resolution for them and help them see that anger doesn't need to escalate.

At the midpoint of the continuum are chronic conflicts, smoldering over time. Eventually they tend to move toward the edges of the continuum: either they burn out or they cause the relationship to burn up.

Acute conflicts constitute the opposite pole from minor disagreements. These powerful expressions of anger can destroy years of love, and they can leave participants (and property) shattered. Regardless of scale, from a marriage to a war, acute conflicts bring emotional and physical devastation—in the worst cases, death.

Practicing mindfulness helps us develop the capacity to recognize the presence of anger and conflict in and around us. This doesn't mean that mindfulness is a remedy for poisonous anger, but it does support applying the antidote of patience. Furthermore, presence of mind supports constructive action. The following scenarios provide examples:

- **You wait in a restaurant for your spouse, who arrives forty minutes late without having updated you.** While waiting, you begin to notice annoyance. You can feed the annoyance with thoughts such as "He's so thoughtless. I can't believe he's kept me waiting, and he didn't even make the time to text or call," "She takes me for granted and probably decided that talking with her friend was more important than getting here on time," or "Maybe he got into an accident and is dying in the street!" Or you can notice what's happening and allow the prickles of annoyance to pass because *they are just thoughts and feelings*; you really don't know what happened, so these suppositions are empty. Then once he or she arrives, you can respond effectively to the real circumstances. Consider: your annoyance only causes you suffering—he or she doesn't feel it—and angry reactions spawned by annoyance generally backfire rather than catalyze positive change.

■ **Your partner once again does something you've repeatedly asked him or her not to do:** maybe leaving dirty clothes on the floor, bringing colleagues home from work and leaving a mess in the kitchen for you to clean up, failing to show up (again) for an important event, or spending a lot of money despite your desire to save. These actions easily trigger feelings of anger. Without mindfulness, you might lose your temper. But if you're familiar with mindfulness, you can Pause instead.

Compare the results: a miserable argument or an opportunity to promote change in a constructive manner. Which feels better for you—and your spouse? Which is most likely to produce the desired outcomes? It's so easy to give in to the temptation of striking out in anger, and thereby risk escalating the situation.

Training your attention and awareness improves your ability to witness your emotions mindfully; this, in turn, increases your capacity to respond reasonably to triggers, rather than react angrily.

■ **You suspect your spouse is having an affair.** Maybe you find evidence, or a friend relates details about a suspicious encounter between your spouse and an attractive stranger. Your thoughts are likely to start racing, either rejecting the possibility of an affair or connecting the dots among seemingly confirmatory data. Emotions generally follow. Perhaps you decide on an explanation that primes you to rage accusatorially at him or her; perhaps you rally supportively to his or her side. Bringing mindfulness to this situation can help you distinguish between reality and supposition, suspicion and trust. Falsely accusing your spouse is damaging to your relationship and causes unnecessary suffering. Similarly, losing control of your emotions won't ease the pain of discovering that your fears are well founded.

- **You're tempted into having an affair.** Maybe you've grown apart and have tried unsuccessfully to resuscitate the freshness of what you once had. You have a boring yet comfortable life together, including a stable family structure for the kids and shared property. But inside, you're slowly suffocating, and your spouse hasn't ever noticed. So when you feel a connection with someone else (someone who you believe truly "sees you"), you're tempted. Maybe you fantasize about this person while having sex with your spouse, or you bring your fantasies to life. Perhaps this new passion involves the soul mate you've looked for all your life and marks the end of an already doomed marriage. Or perhaps not. Maybe the affair isn't a "keeper" but it's still nice, or maybe having the affair actually reaffirms your commitment to your marriage.

  Regardless, mindfulness will help you see what's happening clearly so you know exactly what you're doing—and risking. So much infidelity "just happens": someone attends a conference, has a few drinks at the bar, and ends up spending the night in a stranger's room. The point here is to be mindful of your marriage, your longings, and your desires, and to make active choices about your actions—don't let it "just happen."

- **You're happily married and then, out of the blue, your spouse tells you he or she found someone else or is ready to disclose a different sexual orientation.** This is a major trigger, loaded with diverse and powerful emotions. Experiencing these feelings is natural and inevitable, but your mindfulness training will measurably impact your ability to manage them—rather than relinquish control to them. You're likely to feel intense anger, but remaining mindful of your anger can help you work with it. Maybe you feel that you have a right to give in to your rage, but your "rights" and even the "rightness of those emotions" won't solve the problem.

What do you do? First you Pause, and then you Pause again. You notice your racing thoughts and raging emotions, and you decide what *you need to do in that moment to take care of yourself.* Then you act on that decision, and allow yourself time to process what's happening, so your next steps are as constructive as possible: for yourself, your kids (if relevant), and your marriage.

Sharing your life with a partner can be the cause of infinite love and pleasure; it can also lead to anger and despair. There are diverse conflicts in every marriage, and there's really no way to prepare for their specific circumstances. However, bringing mindfulness to anger and conflict—at any stage—can slow its spread. Mindfulness creates conditions that aren't conducive to anger. But if anger sparks, the practice of mindfulness functions as a flame retardant, protecting and preventing the spread of anger and helping to dampen, if not extinguish, it. Later, mindfulness can be a mental salve, cooling and healing what's been scorched.

MINDFULNESS OF A FAILING RELATIONSHIP

Knowing the nature of your relationship is critically important for taking responsibility about how you live in it. This includes how you handle conflict, disappointment, and the recognition that what you have isn't what you want. Although mindfulness is not the answer to an unfulfilling relationship, it can help you find your own answers and also seek professional or ministerial support. An infusion of help from a trustworthy third-party, such as a therapist or religious leader, can frequently help married couples move beyond their ruts. If your marriage is in trouble, and you haven't already sought help, I strongly encourage you to do so.

Whatever course you take, you're likely to realize eventually that none of us can force anyone else to change; we can only control whether or not we change our own perspective and behaviors. Examine your own role in the marriage, as well as your spouse's. See if there are areas of your own experience, attitudes, and behavior that can change for the better before trying to get your spouse to change. It's far easier to motivate and sustain your own growth than another person's.

Frequently, however, one partner's growth and constructive changes prompt the other to follow intuitively. This is a much subtler but far more potent approach than trying to force someone else to make changes. One of two things will happen if you do everything possible *within yourself* to improve your relationship: either the relationship will improve, or it won't. And if it doesn't get better, you will have far greater confidence in your assessment that there's nothing more to be done.

If you want to end the relationship, mindfulness can help you do so as compassionately and carefully as possible. The first step is acknowledging where you are. From there, you can begin to consider your options and evaluate the relative merits of different strategies. Sometimes a marriage or other serious relationship appears on the brink of disaster but can still be salvaged by shared motivation and effort. If you don't try to save it, you risk wondering *whether you could have* sometime later. On the other hand, you might have already exhausted all the possible remedies and reached the conclusion that there's nothing left to save. If so, then your responsibility shifts to determining how best to minimize the conflict and potential for damage that comes with breaking intimate ties.

RIDING THE WAVES

Significant, intimate relationships enrich our lives. Healthy couples share conditions that promote greater empathy and resilience, and contented partners tend to feel stronger and more effective because together they are more than they would be apart. Knowing that you are fundamentally happy together can enhance your contentment. Kindness nourishes strong relationships, and joy breeds greater joy.

Although the future typically looks rosy at the dawn of a new romance, the promise of happiness is not a guarantee of success. There are always ups and downs in relationships, but how we ride the waves contributes to their shape in the future. With greater mindfulness and kindness, the ups can get higher and longer while the downs become more shallow and less frequent. In contrast, the presence (and escalation) of anger and conflict reverses this trend.

All relationships—like waves of water or the brainwaves that support the functioning of the mind—change.

9 • Mindfulness at Work

CULTIVATING MINDFULNESS at work might seem less compelling than being mindful with your spouse or partner, or less pleasurable than practicing Mindful Sex, but it's equally as important. Mindfulness in the workplace can greatly enhance your performance, improve your relations with coworkers, and reduce workplace-related stress—improving quality of life for you, your coworkers, your clients, and everyone.

We spend an enormous amount of time working—for our livelihood, as students, or in service as volunteers, and so your feelings about your job have a huge effect on your overall emotional life. It's important for your well-being that your work doesn't repulse you or conflict with your core beliefs. Beyond that baseline, you might also seek meaningful employment that enables you to make a contribution to your community or in the world at large. But regardless of what you do for a living, every job has its share of stressors and unpleasantness, which mindfulness can help mitigate.

You're already familiar with several mindfulness techniques that are applicable to work settings. These include Pause, Mindful Thinking, and Mindfulness of Emotions. This chapter addresses multiple ways to work them into your experience on the job. In addition, the following pages adapt Sharing Kindness practice to work.

TWO TYPES OF PRACTICE

Basic mindfulness techniques are preparation—not proxies—for the spontaneity of life.

With increased familiarity, you're likely to practice without consciously thinking of the technique. In this way, your experience of mindfulness broadens and your sensitivity extends beyond the specific object of any particular technique.

Formal mindfulness practices utilize discrete techniques involving specific steps and instructions. They're called "formal" because practicing in this way is identifiable amid your regular activities; essentially, you follow the steps deliberately and intentionally, rather than spontaneously and naturally. Unpremeditated practice is called "informal practice."

The nominal outcomes of formal practice are arbitrary and artificial. For example, there is no inherent value to counting your breaths; the point is not to become a better counter. Similarly, the desired outcome of Mindful Breathing is a well-trained mind, not being a better breather.

Formal practice supports informal practice; as your formal practice strengthens, you'll be more able to apply mindfulness in the midst of regular life. There will always be boundaries that distinguish formal practice from informal practice, but these borders will soften over time as you move back and forth. In other words, you don't suddenly switch from formal practice to informal practice. Rather you'll learn to shift smoothly and automatically between these two types of practice, just as you change gears in a familiar car.

The process of training with a specific mindfulness technique is *practice*, in the most literal sense of the word. Just as we do when learning to drive, we begin in a safe, quiet place, when we're not rushing or flustered. Developing and internalizing skills in this deliberate way prepares us to bring mindfulness into less controlled circumstances—perhaps, for instance, you Pause rather than simply react in the midst of an intense situation.

Informal practice is far more active than formal practice; it's applied mindfulness, and it's challenging. However, regularly engaging in formal practice makes it much easier to integrate mindfulness within fluid experience. Formal practice keeps you mentally fit, just as ongoing physical training allows athletes to stay strong and ready for competition. Also, your experience of formal practice will deepen as your informal practice expands. As mindfulness proves increasingly relevant through lived experience, you're likely to find that your commitment and motivation also improves.

Changing Gears

Applying mindfulness in daily life is a lot like driving a car—the process involves changing gears.

Neutral

Practicing mindfulness in neutral is doing so with an external prompt: when a teacher instructs you to, when your partner or coworker reminds you to, when you follow the steps in this book. Just as a car can roll in neutral when given a push, so too does mindfulness move in you in neutral.

Don't confuse practicing in neutral with ignorance about mindfulness. There's nothing wrong with neutral; it's where we all begin.

First Gear

You've moved beyond neutral when your own internal cues motivate you to practice mindfulness. Typically this happens under more or less optimal conditions: when you feel relaxed (or at least, not especially pressured) and you make or find the time for practicing. For example, you might dedicate thirty seconds to practicing a particular mindfulness technique during your lunch break. Many people find practicing at work somewhat easier than at home, if only because the boundaries between responsibilities are clear: taking a little time for yourself during a break at work is sanctioned. In contrast, if you have kids, family, chores, etc. at home, you might not rest during your "down time."

Routines at work can support integrating mindfulness into your daily experience. For example, you might take thirty seconds for Mindful Breathing when you first arrive at work, during a lunch or bathroom break, or when you prepare to leave at the end of the day.

Likewise, you could make time for practice once you finish your commute or as you wait to close shop.

Applying mindfulness in first gear means *remembering* to pay attention to your present-moment experience. This is mindfulness at the macro level: remaining mindful of mindfulness. Once you remember your goal of bringing mindfulness into your daily life, you can more easily transition to the microlevel practice by training with a particular technique.

There are multiple options for integrating time for formal practice within a regular workday. Your overall routine won't change, but what you do during those thirty-second intervals will be different: in that brief time, you'll switch your attention from the job-related thoughts, speech, and actions so you can focus on cultivating mindfulness. First gear moves mindfulness into daily life, and it's appropriate to begin very slowly.

Second Gear

As mindfulness begins to move in the flow of your daily experience, you progress above first gear. The remaining gears are distinguishable from each other by the intensity of situations and the skill with which you are able to remain mindful during them. For example, in second gear, which is still a low gear, you might notice when something at work triggers a mild emotion. Perhaps the emotion is pleasant, such as feeling excited and pleased by a compliment or when trusted with greater responsibility. Alternatively, you might feel uncomfortable, slightly threatened, irritated, or even envious. Applying mindfulness in second gear involves recognizing that you feel something a little bit more intensely than normal and having the capacity to simultaneously experience the emotion and witness it.

In second gear, you might notice that you feel excited because you are able to make better-than-expected progress yet frustrated that your coworkers are slower. Noticing enthusiasm and frustration can cue you to Pause (perhaps repeatedly) so that your annoyance doesn't spoil your pleasure. Or you might have a relatively minor difference of opinion with a coworker, but you remain mindful that you can live with the outcome either way. In this case, applying Pause (once or more) to better modulate your emotion will help you contain the conflict and discuss your differences constructively.

Third Gear

This level involves moderate experiences and emotions. Things happen faster and more dynamically than in second gear, and there are more variables at play. In other words, the stakes are higher—but not very. Applying mindfulness in third gear means staying present so that emotions don't propel you into a situation before you really take the time to consider the implications: during a heated but controlled conflict with your boss or an employee you supervise, for instance. At this level you watch the situation unfold, notice what happens in and around you, and recognize whether you see old familiar patterns repeating.

Remaining mindful in such situations facilitates better outcomes, for you and the other person. If the emotion is desirable, you can enjoy it fully without developing unrealistic expectations based on the circumstances. If it's destructive, you have a greater capacity for forming a constructive response rather than reacting disproportionately.

Over time, you'll recognize how dynamics escalate—for better or worse—and Pause earlier and earlier. In this cause, applying Pause won't diminish your enthusiasm for a new, exciting, and possibly risky opportunity; rather, you'll savor it more. Likewise, remaining mindful will increase your resilience: you won't become as upset, or remain rattled as long, as you did in the past. Other people are likely to notice the difference and might comment, "You're a lot less reactive than before," or ask, "How did you manage to stay calm?"

Fourth Gear

In fourth gear, you have intense experiences; they last a while, and their effects often linger and change the direction or tone of relationships. A positive fourth-gear experience at work might be the exhilaration of working closely with another person and together succeeding at your task despite long odds. That process produces an intense bond, and together you glory in the ephemeral euphoria of accomplishment. Afterward, ordinary life often seems like a letdown; it's boring or even depressing. Less desirable fourth-gear experiences include handling the hurt, anger, and disappointment that come when a trusted colleague deeply insults or betrays you. In these instances, your body and mind go into stress mode, and they tempt you to react aggressively or run away. However, neither reaction bodes well.

Applying mindfulness to fourth-gear situations slows things down so you're better able to observe the complicated dynamics at play. You'll breathe and watch, so you can feel your feelings and witness their motion. Remaining mindful allows you to manage your emotions consciously and consequently improve the chances of a useful or positive outcome. The point is to stay mindful during the instant at which a trigger throws you powerfully onto a particular mental, emotional, or behavioral trajectory, and then sustain mindfulness while journeying in that direction.

Fifth Gear

At this level, you bring mindfulness into the most intense situations: major life changes and challenges. These can include experiences of ecstasy and profound, positive, spiritual transformations. The other end of the continuum includes divorce, loss of an important job, and death of a loved one. Fifth-gear conditions tend to inform your life for a significant period of time, and they alter your daily experience profoundly. Regardless of whether they occur at home, in relationships, or at work, they spill over into every other important aspect of your life. In fifth gear, there is no separation between professional life and personal life.

Applying mindfulness in fifth gear means you stay absolutely present, regardless of how ecstatic or searing an experience might be. You don't "check out" or go numb, and neither do you allow yourself to be swept up in euphoria. Rather, you maintain awareness that there is more to you, and your life, than the specific dynamics at play. Painful fifth-gear situations won't cause you to lose hope, because you will have unshakable confidence that everything changes. Blissful fifth-gear occurrences won't cause you to become disappointed when life returns to normal. Whatever is happening, and whatever happens, mindfulness supports you in being present each step of the way.

The one gear not present in this metaphor is reverse; I believe that mindfulness practice does not permit anyone to go backward. Sure, you can slow down your practice, and even shift into neutral and coast to a stop, but you can't undo the "aha" moments that come with mindfulness practice. You will always know that *mindfulness is experientially different from mindlessness.* The same is true for having tasted hot crusty bread fresh from the oven after a lifetime of eating prepackaged loaves. You might not get another chance to visit that bakery again, but you'll know without certainty that all bread is not equal.

With mindfulness, the radical shift lies in recognizing that you can pay attention to attention and develop awareness of awareness; once you know this, ignorance is no longer available. Furthermore, as you become increasingly familiar with applying mindfulness along the continuum of intensity, you gain a more expansive and accurate appreciation for the difference mental training can make.

Just as cars can't go from neutral to fifth gear directly, few if any of us can transition from the formal practice of mindfulness techniques to applying mindfulness confidently and skillfully in the midst of a life-changing event. We've got to develop our capacity by bringing mindfulness to experiences that are incrementally more challenging. This takes time. If you're just beginning to explore mindfulness now, remember to be gentle with yourself and have reasonable expectations. If you've been practicing mindfulness for a long time, you'll already know through experience that being aware of "losing it" (regardless of whether the situation is marked by destructive or desirable emotions) is still an experience of mindfulness. Mindful living takes a lifetime, but practicing is a moment-by-moment decision.

WHERE IS YOUR MIND?

Redundant though it sounds, *mindfulness practice requires being mindful* of taking the time to practice, remembering and applying the techniques, and then returning your attention back to ordinary life. For this, you need to pay attention to the circumstances, goals, and activities related to mindfulness practice in the midst of other mental activities and distractions. This is particularly clear in the workplace, where you are responsible for engaging in very specific tasks and have to manage the potential for distractions.

Training your attention to *repeatedly return to where you want it* is the solution to many work-related challenges. Consider: can you focus adequately on particular tasks that you really enjoy or find interesting? Perhaps. But do you become distracted if you feel bored or dislike your task—even if you're required to accomplish it? If so, improving your ability to return your attention to specific objects is important. Even more important, though, is the ability to sharpen your awareness so you know if/when you lose focus.

Imagine: you're at work, sitting at your desk, perhaps staring out the window. Or at least your body is doing so; your mind is elsewhere. Your attention is engaged somewhere, but you may not even realize that your focus has shifted from your work. Your awareness is missing in action. If you don't notice that you've become distracted, you won't know that you need to bring your mind back into focus. This puts you at risk for missing opportunities as well as being called to account by a coworker or your boss.

Mental distraction at work poses two significant issues. In the first place, your work will suffer if you're not present—in mind as in body—on the job. For example, you might lose track of the number of items you've counted and have to start over. Or you might realize that you wandered off topic in a report that you're writing because a minor facet interested you more than the main point. Either way, you have to go back and redo (or at least recheck) your work, and this adds time.

Additionally, the more often your mind wanders down a certain path, the more likely it is to head down that path again. For instance, perhaps you occasionally allow yourself to browse online shopping at work. The more often you let yourself do this, the more often you'll find yourself wondering what sales you can find today, and the more time you will spend (or waste) thinking about it. And if your mental wandering takes you into unpleasant feelings and destructive thoughts, you're reinforcing mental habits that increase suffering.

Mental distraction can be internally generated or externally cued. Sometimes our thoughts manage to take our attention on a mental detour. This happens when we're in the middle of doing something, and all of a sudden our minds generate a compelling thought—maybe a question or an answer. Once noticed, the new train of thought beckons our minds to follow it, and off we go, somewhere other than the present.

The same dynamic occurs when you're working in the presence of other people, and their speech, appearance, or behavior grabs your attention and holds it. If you're lucky, the people move on quickly, and you return to your task without much disruption. But often, they linger—in person or in your mind. Maybe you overheard something interesting, exciting, or upsetting before the people moved on. They planted a seed in your mind, and it starts to germinate. Over time, the subsequent sequence of new thoughts draws you further away from your original task.

Unproductive mental habits can also negatively impact your future. If your boss notices that you're distracted, you might be reprimanded. If you can't get your work done during normal business hours, you might need to stay later, which cuts into your personal time. If the quality of your performance suffers overall, you might be passed over for promotion. The possibilities are endless, but they are connected by a lack of awareness of wandering attention.

As you've seen in earlier chapters, mindfulness training increases mental fitness by focusing attention and strengthening awareness. We may imagine attention is "sexier." You place your attention volitionally, and then carry on accordingly. But though it may seem less compelling, I believe that awareness is the key. Awareness lets you know when you've lost focus, be it on a particular work-related task or on the all-encompassing effort to bring mindfulness into your daily life. With greater awareness, you know if you're paying attention to your attention, and if not, awareness reminds you to refocus.

WHEN YOU LOOK, SEE

Awareness is also the key to experiencing people, events, problems, or opportunities freshly. You can place your attention on anyone or anything, but looking at your object of attention does not mean you automatically see what's there. The idea is to look with openness so you see *who* is there, not *what* you expect. The value of noticing what's right in front of your eyes, and not only what's already in your mind, is basic business practice and applies to all professions.

Prejudging a client walking in the door, a patient sitting in an exam room, a potential customer, or a colleague can be disastrous—regardless of whether your projections are positive or negative. Of course, there is much to be gained from looking at someone to glean data with which to make associations, and on which to base actions. But analysis follows observation, and direct experience should precede observation. That is, you should see the person before you see the client, patient, customer, or colleague. It means you have an open gaze, so that you can notice whatever appears, before you start thinking about what you see.

In the workplace, making an incorrect assumption after a first glance can have tremendous ripple effects. If you decide to trust someone based on appearance or demeanor, you risk discovering that your trust is misplaced. Alternatively, you can miss valuable opportunities when you dismiss someone based on similar criteria. Consider the retail clerk who misjudges a customer—as wealthy or not—and wastes time or, worse, loses a major sale. Likewise, a doctor might make a simple diagnosis based on a patient's obvious symptoms and miss the subtle but dangerous underlying condition. The same thing applies for quick assessments of new team members: seeing only what you are habituated to see severely limits your possibilities.

But simply understanding this concept is insufficient; knowing is

MINDFULNESS AT WORK • 135

not the same as doing. Reinforcing desired behavior or altering less constructive habits requires dedication and ongoing practice. So when you first look up at someone else (or even in that first instant when you see your own face in a mirror), apply mindfulness and notice whether you pay attention to seeing, first, before thinking about what you see.

The sequence that begins with seeing, moves through thinking (and analyzing), and takes you to action is frequently rapid. Buying a little time can make all the difference in your ultimate assessment and judgment. Using Pause when you first look at someone can help. So when the client, patient, customer, or colleague first catches your attention, switch to taking a mindful breath, and then return to the person. Notice what you see as you return your attention, and then carry on as normal. In this scenario, the arrival of a person cues your mindfulness practice, and using the technique positions your brain to process what you see more mindfully.

The same strategy applies to your initial encounters with nonliving things, including places, things, and ideas. If you're a builder, you can train your mind to see *place* before *building site*. If you travel for work, you can Pause before you walk into an appointment or meeting. You are somewhere, physically, no matter what you do; the idea is to pay attention to being aware of your location. You can do the same thing with ideas and information. People who "think outside the box" demonstrate the ability to see possibility and opportunity when others don't. Put differently, they don't structure data according to conventional labels, or at least not so as to exclude other options. A "useless piece of junk" to one person might be "just what was needed" to someone else. Likewise, a seemingly irrelevant idea might hold the answer to an otherwise intractable problem.

However, while staying present with new people, in a new location, or with new information has its own challenges, it's far easier than remaining mindful when your work becomes automatic. The problem is that most jobs involve repetitive work to some degree. Writers use different words in each sentence but type using the same letters. Likewise, surgeons operate on unique individual patients, but they use the same procedures over and over again. The risk comes when the numbness of familiarity and skill means you fail to recognize the newness of each instant or situation. Therefore, mindfulness practice is protective.

These same dynamics are central to mindful leadership. This is not to say that all effective leaders are necessarily mindful in the broad sense we've explored throughout this book. But the fresh clarity and sharp focus that comes with mindfulness certainly enhances leadership. Effective leaders pay attention and have excellent situational and internal awareness. They are sensitive to the ups and downs of the business climate as well as the workplace climate. They notice their own perceptions and actions, and they recognize other people's needs, goals, and motivations. More than anything else, skilled leaders can manage their own emotions, think clearly and critically, and perform under pressure. The benefits of mindfulness practice are as relevant for professional leadership as they are for employees, at work as at home.

KINDNESS AT WORK

People work better when they're happy—or at least content. So cultivating kindness at work, for coworkers, clients, patients, or customers, is worthwhile just as it is at home, with family or close friends.

You can share kindness at work through overt actions. However, the range of expression for sharing kindness in the workplace is limited to appropriate and sanctioned interactions. Few of us can, or would want to, hug the boss. But all of us can make eye contact and smile.

Likewise, verbal acknowledgments of your coworkers' humanity are expressions of kindness. Purposefully and specifically greeting others—even those with whom you don't directly work, such as the mailman or the boss—can enrich both of your experiences. Similarly, there's kindness in the generosity that motivates you to bring a cup of coffee to a coworker when you return with your own. Simply asking "How are you?" and listening to the response is an act of kindness. So too is asking after someone's family or health. You can share kindness in similar ways even when you only communicate by telephone or email. The point is to make the effort to engage person-to-person.

Inner gestures of kindness include consciously hoping the best for someone, even when you have concerns or disagree with their position. Recognizing your own feelings of animosity or anger, such as when you feel wronged or slighted, and refraining from lashing out is also kindness: for yourself and the other person. You contribute to a better working environment when you remain patient or choose to express your emotions constructively when frustrated by a coworker's actions or inaction. The basic ingredients of a healthy work climate are safety, respect, and fairness. The spice is kindness, and adding it to the mix makes all the difference.

Basic expressions of kindness in the work environment are relevant even when you communicate across distances, by telephone or electronically. Perhaps its harder to remember civility outside of face-to-face encounters, when the other person seems more like an object (or obstacle) than a living, breathing human just like you. However, there are two main reasons to infuse your email and telephone communications with kindness. First, *you will feel better* when you interact with a real person, and treating that person with kindness is an implicit reminder and recognition that you're engaging with someone, not something. In addition, your interactions will be smoother and more constructive when neither of you feel disrespected or demeaned. Investing in the human process of working together typically yields better, more valuable, and more efficient outcomes. There is a disproportionately high return on investment associated with offering small, but genuine, gestures of kindness whenever and wherever possible.

Sharing kindness with someone you like probably feels more natural than purposefully bringing kindness into interactions with people you dislike. However, you don't have to like coworkers to treat them politely. In fact, kindness is not the same as friendship—or love. Rather, it's a quality that tempers behaviors so that you act from a position of strength and clarity. Expressing kindness is a stronger indicator of your integrity than a reflection of the other person's character.

Indeed, another difference between Sharing Kindness at work versus at home is that at work you generate feelings of kindness for people with whom you have much less intimate relationships. Remember, kindness is the desire that other people experience happiness. You don't have to be an active participant in their happiness, but you can still wish the best for them. Doing so actually increases your own happiness and sense of well-being. Superficially, kindness benefits others, but at the deepest level, sharing kindness has an even greater positive impact on your own happiness.

Generating and extending kindness defines how you hold yourself in relation to others, no matter the circumstances of your interactions. Nevertheless, purposefully cultivating kindness is easiest to practice when you can direct your feelings of kindness toward specific people. Coworkers or colleagues that you respect and like provide an excellent target for kindness practice on the job.

To begin, choose one person at work ("X"). You don't need to know the person well, or feel close to him or her, but you should feel some kind of positive connection. Then, practice the steps for **Sharing Kindness at Work** to support your experience in the workplace by (1) sharing kindness with a coworker and (2) becoming familiar with the technique so that you can use it *at work*.

- **Focus** your attention on experiencing kindness and extending kindness from your heart toward X.
- **Observe** with awareness whether you stay focused on experiencing and extending kindness to X or whether you become distracted.
- **Refocus** your attention, if needed.

Next, identify someone at work toward whom you have essentially neutral feelings ("Y"): maybe a security guard who lets you into the building but with whom you don't otherwise interact, a new employee, or a senior boss you never see. Now repeat Sharing Kindness at Work toward that person.

- **Focus** your attention on experiencing kindness and extending kindness from your heart toward Y.
- **Observe** with awareness whether you stay focused on experiencing and extending kindness to Y or whether you become distracted.
- **Refocus** your attention, if needed.

Finally, if you feel ready, take this technique one step further by practicing it toward someone at work you don't like. It's best to begin with someone you only mildly dislike, but then, over time, you might choose to practice Sharing Kindness at Work toward people you really feel antipathy. Just remember that all of us suffer in some way and that the people we dislike, like us, are also hurting. While on the job, it's hard to feel happy inside yourself when you have to work with unhappy people.

So if you want to be even happier at work, it's only logical to make a little effort to send kindness to your unhappy coworkers. Furthermore, generating kindness feels good for the giver, regardless of whether the object of Sharing Kindness ever receives the gift. It's a kind of strategic altruism; you practice because it's good for you, and by extension, others.

Sharing Kindness is not about forgiveness. The point is not to form a friendship with someone you previously disliked. Rather, the purpose is fourfold: (1) to increase your capacity for cultivating and extending kindness; (2) to experience the pleasure of Sharing Kindness, which contributes to your own happiness; (3) to strengthen your understanding that your own happiness is linked to other people's; and (4) to spread happiness to others, through your own increased emotional well-being.

WHERE WORK ENDS

This chapter covered many different angles related to bringing mindfulness into the workplace. We transitioned between formal and informal practice, and back again (and again), in the effort to see how mindful living is both the practice and the purpose of training the mind to be present. We also extended the experience of Sharing Kindness into the workplace, to coworkers—those we like, those we feel neutral toward, and even those we dislike. Sharing Kindness, like other mindfulness practices, directly benefits the practitioner but also ripples outward into relationships and community.

In addition to improving your performance through training attention and awareness, mental training can also increase your happiness in the workplace and in your overall life. Not only do we spend an enormous amount of time at work, but the workday experience easily impacts what happens at home or at play. As this chapter shows, being more mindful at work is clearly good for your career. In the next chapter, we'll explore using these same mental skills to help you leave your career at work and be present with friends and family at home.

10 • Mindful Parenting

MINDFUL PARENTING is the most effective and natural approach to raising mindful children.

Just consider, what do children seek from their parents? The answer is simple: they want our full attention, right then and there. Fulfilling this desire is a profound expression of love that then creates shared experience. Loving your children and feeling their love in return comes with real presence.

The point is this: there's nothing exotic about training your mind to be present with your children. You already know how to begin, and this chapter will take you one step further through exploring mindfulness in the context of parenting.

However, before we become immersed in practical applications for mindful parenting, there are two important themes to consider. First, mindful parenting relies on *your* mindfulness practice—it's not about finding mindfulness programs for your kid. This is especially important to consider now, as programs, books, and other resources on raising mindful kids proliferate.

I wonder whether kids are able to experience mindfulness, so long before their brains mature. Sure they can appear mindful—or at least present—with their immediate experience, but I doubt they are aware of the quality of their attention (at least, not in the same way as adults). At a superficial level, kids are clearly able to follow basic mindfulness techniques and derive benefit from self-calming and relaxation skills. However, those outcomes are not synonymous with experiencing or demonstrating mindfulness. And forcing kids to (appear to) be mindful "for their own good" may turn them off, leaving them unlikely to explore the practice later in life.

Secondly, mindfulness is not a panacea for every challenge that confronts parents and their children. There are more pressing priorities than practicing mindfulness, despite the possible benefits—when health and well-being are severely compromised, for instance. Furthermore, mindfulness is not enough even when the challenges are less severe, such as with generally healthy kids who have issues with attention or depression. If this is your reality, practicing mindfulness can certainly help you become a more effective advocate for your child, but you also need to seek clinical assistance for him or her.

Mindful parenting is simultaneously altruistic toward your children and in your self-interest. Parents that notice and nurture their children provide them with fundamental advantages that support child development. Children thrive with close, stable attachment; numerous studies demonstrate that lack of nurture predisposes children to suffering from increasing psychological and physical disorders in adulthood. And, as every parent knows, when you become a parent, your happiness joins inextricably with your children's, so happy children means happier parents.

Mindful parenting involves making hard choices, steadfastly offering loving protection, providing supportive guidance, and giving compassion, especially regarding discipline. As you'll see in the following pages, mindfulness is good for parents and children in myriad ways.

Although the strict definition of being a parent is specific to biology, the relationship of parenting encompasses a far broader spectrum of possibilities. Furthermore, even well into adulthood, many of us seek out surrogate parents when our biological parents are unavailable (for any number of possible reasons). Therefore, the basic tenets of mindful parenting apply to people who take a *parenting role* in relationship with someone—regardless of whether that person is a blood relative. This chapter on mindfulness and parenting is relevant for anyone who fills this role, regardless of blood.

You're the Parent

Although kids seem to live in the present, they go through daily life without being consciously aware of paying attention to their present-moment experience. Consider a toddler, who totally focuses on one thing, only to switch her attention completely to something else. Her immediate focus looks mindful, but really it's just that her brain handles only one source of stimulation at a time—and when something new grabs her attention, the prior activity is out of sight and out of mind. Perhaps one reason we so enjoy sharing kids' natural present-ness is that parenting allows us to re-experience the simple focus and wonder of childhood without having the brain of a child.

The fact that parents are adults, and children are not, is really the key to understanding mindful parenting. We can practice mindfulness, and they can benefit from the conditions we create. Growing up with love—expressed by full attention, empathy, and compassion—prepares kids to make healthy decisions about mind and body when they reach adulthood.

What we do is far more powerful than what we say. If you want to promote mindfulness, then behave mindfully. Be careful with what you say, and how you manage your emotions. And while it's true that your ten-year-old probably won't make a conscious connection between your mindfulness practice and your ability to stay calm under pressure, the same child at seventeen will probably understand. However, even very young children instinctively feel the difference between mindful and nonmindful parenting. Seeing how mindfulness facilitates desirable outcomes is the most potent justification for developing these specific skills. Kids (like adults) have little motivation to train in mindfulness simply because it's good for them. But mindfulness becomes interesting and valuable when they see that practicing makes life easier, more enjoyable, and more successful.

On the other hand, if you "talk the talk" without "walking the walk" your kids will know. Kids watch us all the time, and they have an extraordinary capacity for recognizing inconsistency. They notice when adults mindlessly promote the importance of mindfulness. This is doubly harmful for them, because not only do they feel disappointed by the hypocrisy, they also make negative associations with mindfulness that might prevent them from exploring the practice under better circumstances later in life.

Our kids want us to be the best parents possible *for them;* we don't need to be perfect. In fact, they need us to show them how to manage challenges and handle disappointments as much as they want us to demonstrate success. The idea is to be mindful of what happens in real life and respond constructively. If you feel angry with your kid, knowing that you feel angry in that moment might help you handle the situation more effectively. Likewise, if you feel really frustrated with something other than your child (the traffic, a broken appliance, your job), mindfulness might help you express that frustration appropriately instead of displacing it onto your family. By enhancing your ability to manage strong emotions more effectively, mindfulness actually helps minimize uncomfortable feelings such as shame, regret, and guilt.

BECOMING A PARENT

When you choose to become a parent, you affirm life: both by bringing a new being into the world and trusting that the world (and the child) will be welcoming. You also accept that having and raising children carries enormous potential both for pleasure and for pain. Since the specific joys of parenting are widely celebrated and generally obvious, this chapter focuses on enhancing your experience as a parent by minimizing or mitigating the challenges and suffering associated with childrearing.

In other words, I want to make the lows of your parenting life less low. Picture a line graph showing the waves of emotions in your life: the tops of the curves are the highs, and the bottoms are the points of greatest suffering. Parenting carries us up and down to both extremes, even if daily life generally hovers around a neutral, middle line.

There are two approaches to shifting your quality of life: you can raise the top of the swells, so pleasure becomes more intense; or you can raise the troughs, so pain is less unmanageable and destructive. Both are valid and rewarding, but making the low points less low is more effective, because you decrease the intensity of extreme pain. Mindfulness practice helps make those troughs more shallow, without denying or diminishing the suffering that comes with parenting.

There are three types of pain associated with parenting:

1. The pure and simple physical pain associated with bearing and raising kids.
2. The ache that comes from wanting what you cannot give your kids; this could include tangible belongings and wealth or specific skills and characteristics—or both. Another form of this is wishing them to be free of burdens they have to bear.
3. The suffering that comes with worrying about what could go wrong and what you might lose.

Of these, the first is physical, whereas the other two are mental and emotional. And yet the mindfulness-based strategies to handle, minimize, or eliminate suffering are remarkable consistent, regardless of the type of pain.

What Hurts?

With parenting, joy and pain are inextricably linked, and they start well before the actual birth: as soon as pre-parents begin thinking about a child, or when they learn of pregnancy. Longing for a child is a mixture of anticipated happiness and the discomfort of uncertain outcomes. Then, the process of carrying a fetus brings a mix of sensations and emotions—for the mother, obviously, but also experienced uniquely by the other parent. For example, the feeling of a fetus moving within you is hard to understand unless you've lived it or felt it happening within someone else. It brings paradoxical feelings of bliss, because *someone is in there*, and pain, when *it* kicks hard or hooks a foot under your rib. Similarly, giving birth is miraculous and messy; most of us experience an indescribable pleasure of welcoming a child into the world—and feel (at least some) excruciating pain during delivery. Both parents can access the same joy and gratitude, and although the mother actually has the physical pain, many fathers suffer profoundly through empathy.

Once delivered, children continue to trigger physical sensations and emotions on both extremes of the continuum. Just as holding a baby in your arms is a precious pleasure, staying up night after night when a baby has colic is tiring and painful. When children are older, the specific circumstances change but the feelings continue. Parents experience a visceral joy watching a child receive an honor at school, win a competition, or simply master the skill of riding a bicycle. Those same parents get headaches and backaches from carrying kids who are too tired to walk, or later, stay up late to make sure homework is completed or a teenager makes it home safely from a party. The list is endless, but the following chart provides some other common examples of the pleasure/pain phenomenon.

Most of these examples are of the first type of suffering associated

PLEASURE	PAIN
Rejoicing in your child's pleasures	Hurting when your child hurts
Having the joyful responsibility of raising a child	Physical exhaustion due to being on call 24/7
Seeing your child crawl or walk for the first time	Changing diapers and cleaning up vomit and all types of messes
Celebrating a child's birthday and milestones of healthy growth	Exhaustion from caring for sick children and getting their colds too
Hanging out with your child, sharing family time and recreation	Headaches from listening to your child's music (from toddlerhood through teens)
Playing with your child, no matter the age or stage of development	Myriad aches and pains that come with constant activity: from chasing a toddler to taking older kids to after-school activities

with parenting: physical pain. The next two, you'll recall, deal with emotional distress.

The Second Type of Suffering

The second type of suffering relates to wanting what you don't have. We suffer mentally and emotionally—in almost all life arenas—when we feel that something desirable is missing.

With regard to parenting, this can begin even before conception if you desperately want a child but are not able to bear one. Once the child is on the way, parents frequently worry about whether the child will be healthy, or of the desired gender. Despite their love and courage, many parents whose children face serious health or mental issues wish that their kids were healthy and "ordinary." Even parents of otherwise healthy children might wish that their kids had more patience, could learn easily and perform better at school, or were more athletic.

In addition to desiring specific attributes for children, suffering comes from wanting things—not just special things, but also basic things. Perhaps a mother is concerned that she doesn't have all the material goods she needs to care for her child. Another parent might lack the resources to provide opportunities for his kids but still have the deep desire to do so. It hurts when you can't send you kid to a special extracurricular event because it's too expensive. Likewise, parents feel pain when their children don't have the same type of clothes, games, sports, or musical equipment as their friends do; we know that kids suffer when they stand out among their peers.

In sum, the possibilities for suffering due to lack are endless, and though the desired object frequently changes over time, the type of suffering continues.

The Third Type of Suffering

The third type of suffering comes with losing, or fearing the loss of, something precious that we already have.

The most significant potential loss is, of course, the loss of life.

As parents, we know that there are no guarantees to life, health, or happiness. We fear learning that *something's happened*, no matter our child's age. When a previously healthy child becomes ill, parents fear a dreaded diagnosis from a doctor. Others worry about the late-night call from law enforcement, or hearing the knock at the door from a somber chaplain and military officer. There is no way to prepare for the fear that comes with having a child, but staying present despite the fear can help.

Parents also fear other losses, such as when a child leaves home voluntarily for school—or involuntarily, perhaps due to custody rights. Time passes, and the growth of a child brings joy along with pangs of nostalgia. It's so easy to wonder "Where has my little boy or girl gone?" or "Why did he or she have to move so far away?" Of course we don't want kids to get stuck at a certain age, but many parents wish that the process could go a little slower so we could better savor the experience. Paradoxically, the same parents might also want to accelerate certain development periods: the terrible twos or adolescence.

Worrying that you've lost time—with your kids, with your families, and in your own life—is a perverse type of mental and emotional torture. Time doesn't stop, for anything or anyone, yet our perspective informs our experience of reality, and we suffer accordingly. Furthermore, culture and community support certain expectations about how *things should be* in families, with children, and as we age. The pressure to compare your life with societal norms is crushing, and individual lives rarely match Hallmark ideals. But knowing this provides insufficient immunity against some kind of sadness when kids are far away on Father's Day or Mother's Day, or on your birthday or their own. Loss, in these scenarios, refers to the discrepancy between *what is* and *what might have been*. Such scenarios present an abstract type of loss, because *what is* simply *is*—without comparison to any imagined or expected alternative. Nevertheless, the sense of loss feels real, no matter its cause.

EMPATHY AND COMPASSION

Loving your child predisposes you to have empathy; you feel his or her pain as if it were your own. So many parents wish they could take on and thereby take away their child's suffering. Although sharing the suffering doesn't actually reduce any of the pain, feeling empathy begins the process.

Empathy is rooted in mindfulness, directly and indirectly, since the capacity for empathy relates to focusing attention and deepening awareness. The direct relationship concerns your ability to notice what's happening in and around other people. Paying very close attention enables you to recognize suffering around you. Empathy appears when you resonate with that suffering and actually experience it within yourself. Mindfulness contributes to knowing, intellectually and viscerally, others' suffering, and in this way promotes empathy directly.

Mindfulness improves your capacity to recognize suffering and cultivate empathy indirectly though increasing your mental and emotional clarity. Practicing mindfulness sensitizes you to recognizing your own inner distraction, which may be due to personal sensations, thoughts, or feelings. Greater mindfulness also brings greater skill at effectively distinguishing between someone else's pain (or issues and needs) and your own. Cultivating empathy is far more challenging when you, yourself, are in emotional distress or when your attention is scattered—especially when you're not fully aware of your own experience.

Mindfulness also promotes compassion, which is defined as the desire to reduce or relieve suffering. Compassion is active. *Feeling your child's pain* (empathy) leads to generating compassion, which in turn is the basis for constructive action. Compassion, unlike empathy, can transform the experience of suffering; it enables you to be present with pain and feel that you can do something, somehow, that helps.

Suffering while doing nothing is far more destructive than purposefully applying compassion in the midst of pain. Compassion won't change the practical reality of horrible situations; it can't stop a child from dying or losing some critically important opportunity. But compassion does alter the experience of facing that reality. No one wants to consider losing a child, but going through that lived nightmare with compassion is the best possible option for parent and child. Likewise, no one wants a child to experience heartbreak, but the only way to offer comfort comes from staying present compassionately.

Compassion benefits everyone. Generating compassion feels good and helps to relieve your own pain or, alternatively, increase your happiness. Receiving compassion likewise brings solace. This applies for cultivating and extending compassion to the people you love most dearly, as well as those toward whom you are neutral or even those you dislike. We're all human beings, capable of changing for the better, and giving—like receiving—compassion facilitates this process.

Compassion, like kindness, leads to more desirable conditions and experience. Whereas kindness promotes happiness, compassion aims to minimize or eliminate the causes of unhappiness. Specific context and each person's baseline experience determines the approach; however, the ultimate result is the same. And, as with kindness, there are two strategies for expressing compassion: overt action and internal gestures.

The initial expression of compassion is the internal gesture of seeing someone else's pain and feeling a desire to reduce his or her suffering. From there, you can *do something* to help someone by offering emotional support or taking action to increase physical comfort. Compassionate actions include simply staying with someone, witnessing their pain and allowing them the time to work with that pain without having to be alone. Other examples of compassionate actions toward your children involve helping them stay calm and focused when they panic about homework or a competition, working through challenges with them, and recognizing their struggles without trying to fix them.

Sometimes compassion is warm and fuzzy, but often it's firm and honest. You express compassion when you intervene to prevent your child from making a major mistake, or when you refrain from escalating a conflict so that your child's anger diffuses more quickly. Compassion includes protecting children from their own impulses when their desires put them at risk. For example, admitting a child suffering with addiction to a rehab facility is an expression of compassion, even though the entire situation is fraught with pain. Compassion also motivates parents to tell kids when their actions are likely to bring undesirable outcomes, even if it means incurring their anger and disappointment. Compassion does not mean indulgence.

As parents, we have the opportunity and responsibility to model compassion. This is easiest when we show our children how to generate and extend compassion toward others. Involve your children when you give to charity. Include them when you make and bring food to those in need. Volunteer side by side with them to give your time and expertise in service.

At a more subtle level, be sure to explain why you have compassion for others, especially in convoluted and confusing circumstances. Take time to emphasize that you can hold people accountable for their actions and still have compassion for them. This is the basis for the philosophy of "disliking the behavior, not the person" approach to discipline, which applies across the continuum of destructive actions, from the most mild to the most heinous. Help your children understand that compassion and justice are linked, and how withholding compassion leads to dehumanizing others, which is the root of violence from bullying to genocide.

The most powerful and most challenging situations during which to model compassion are those that cut you most deeply. Sometimes kids make decisions about their own best interests that may be healthy but nevertheless break our hearts. For example, a child of divorced parents might live with one parent and then choose to live with the other instead. If the choice is best for the child—or at least not harmful— the only constructive response is compassion: for the child having to make such a choice, and for the suffering felt by the parents. There is no compassion in the alternative approach—custody battles, hatred, and anger—despite how much more attractive fighting might be than acquiescing.

SHARING COMPASSION

Sharing Compassion has three components:

- Recognizing the subject's suffering.
- Feeling empathy.
- Consciously cultivating and extending the desire to reduce or eliminate the pain.

The cause of suffering can be whatever is relevant: from physical pain to emotional suffering to mental difficulties. Initially, choose a source of suffering that feels manageable to you, so you can maintain your focus without feeling emotionally or mentally overwhelmed. Later, as you feel more comfortable with the practice, you can increase the magnitude and depth of the suffering toward which you extend compassion.

When practicing Sharing Compassion, you should move through the first and second components fairly quickly, so you spend the majority of your time and effort on the third. Some people work with the process intellectually and send *thoughts of compassion*. Others have a more experiential and visceral practice during which they *feel* sensations of compassion moving outward from the heart. Once you try the technique, you will likely sense which approach feels more natural for you. It's fine to use both, and likewise it's possible to have a unique, personal approach that accomplishes the same purpose. So long as you move through the three steps, you're Sharing Compassion through meditation.

As with Sharing Kindness, a gradient of challenge also exists for Sharing Compassion. With both techniques, the most powerful and challenging opportunities for practice occur when we focus on people we dislike the most. Therefore, one of the best places to begin Sharing Compassion is by generating and extending this specific quality toward your children. If you're not a parent, go ahead and direct compassion toward someone you love deeply. As you'll see, the following format is familiar, but the instructions for **Sharing Compassion** are specific.

- **Focus your attention** on experiencing compassion and extend-ing compassion from your heart toward your child or children.
- **Observe with awareness** whether you stay focused on experi-encing and extending compassion to your child or children, or whether you become distracted.
- **Refocus your attention**, if needed.

When the technique becomes familiar, try adapting it so that your practice aligns with your breath. Inhalations align with empathy, and exhalations align with compassion. This can feel like you *breathe in the other person's pain* and then transform the suffering into compas-sion that you *send to them on your out-breath*. You're not absorbing the suffering. Instead, you are working with it skillfully and symbolically. The idea is to imagine that you draw the pain away from the other person, just as parents wish they could take their children's pain. Then you transform that pain through your desire to reduce the suffering, and extend compassion to the other person. Breathing gives the prac-tice added power, and it boosts your energy. There's no limit on com-passion, and Sharing Compassion won't drain your reserves.

What Can You Do?

Sharing Compassion is relevant in circumstances when you can take action to reduce suffering, as well as when there's very little to be done. The three steps of the technique are equally applicable in both types of situation. First you recognize the suffering, next you feel empathy, and then you do something—either through overt and direct action and/or internally practicing Sharing Compassion. The specifics of the situation determine your options, regardless of whether you face the dull ache of disappointment when your child is mean, the suffering that comes from losing precious time because your work keeps you away, or the searing pain that comes with a lost or injured child.

If a discrete action can remedy the situation, take it. As you've already discovered, the attention and awareness training that come with mind-fulness practice facilitates making an accurate assessment as well as a constructive response. Even as you act, you can also practice Sharing

Compassion in your mind. For example, if your child breaks an arm falling from a play structure, you can mentally send compassion while you stabilize the arm, whisper words of comfort, and call for help. The idea is to breathe in the pain and breathe out compassion, in the midst of taking action. After all, you have to continue breathing in order to be of any help. If you are alive, and breathing, your compassion can ride on your breath.

When overt action can't really reduce the suffering, you can still make an internal gesture of compassion. There's not much you can really do to ease your child's pain over a lost friendship, social rejection, or failed test. Sure, you can talk about it and help your child process the experience, but ultimately, this type of pain only passes with time. However, you can still practice Sharing Compassion, silently, invisibly, in your child's presence or alone. Inhale the pain, transform it, and extend compassion on your exhalation.

Sharing Compassion, in this context, has several benefits. Practicing the technique enables you to do something (even if only mentally) when there's nothing much to do physically or through action. Feeling that you're doing *something* likely reduces your anxiety and internal suffering. This in turn probably helps your child. Furthermore, by helping you stay calm and present, you're much more likely to notice possible options, perspectives, or actions that could contribute positively to the situation. Ultimately, whether you believe that the practice directly reduces your child's immediate suffering is a personal choice. But, regardless, there are other significant justifications for using it.

Sharing Compassion is applied mindfulness and emphasizes the point that "mindfulness" is not a synonym for passivity. There's always something to do, even if it's only staying present with your child (or any suffering person) and Sharing Compassion, so he or she isn't totally alone. Direct action can be constructive, but sometimes trying to fix the situation only makes things worse. Greater insight and skill with managing emotions can help you recognize when your need to make things better does not align with your child's needs. Likewise, parsing out the difference between your child's pain and your own associated suffering is critically important because *you're the parent, and caring for your child comes first.*

DISCIPLINE WITH COMPASSION

Mindfulness supports more effective discipline for two main reasons. The practice helps you become increasingly aware of what's actually happening with your kid and within yourself. This facilitates a more constructive, rather than reactive, response. Becoming more astute allows you to demonstrate greater skill in determining and implementing your intervention. In addition, applying Pause allows both of you a gap of time during which the conflict's momentum can slow. As a result, you create better conditions within which to address your child's conduct.

Finally, mindfulness practice leads to greater emotional balance. This means that you're more likely to pick your battles with greater discernment. Eventually, you'll be likely to engage in fewer conflicts because your perception changes. Events that used to look like conflicts appear with less emotional baggage or assumed difficulties. Therefore, instead of viewing discipline in the context of punishment, you might provide discipline as a strategy for supporting good conduct. This shift is far more than just a question of semantics because your perspective informs action, and your actions teach your children what's right and wrong, constructive or destructive.

Whether your toddler throws a tantrum or your teenager talks back, the most effective response is to Pause and allow yourself time to move past the initial impulse to react. Tantrums, like disrespect, are about pushing limits and getting attention. Bad behavior is destructive, and it doesn't feel good for anyone involved. Kids abandon such behaviors when they prove ineffective. If being polite results in more desirable outcomes, they'll learn manners. However, they make this cause-and-effect connection only when your behavior confirms the preferable approach. If you yell at your screaming toddler (i.e., throw your own tantrum) you reinforce the power of the tantrum. Likewise, if you rapidly reply in kind to your teenager's sarcastic comment, you reinforce the power of language used disrespectfully. Instead, Pause and wait.

Often appearing to do nothing (which is what applying Pause or Sharing Compassion looks like to others) is the most effective way to capture your kids' attention. They expect a reaction, and they become curious when you take the time to observe. Kids often act out due to a less-than-obvious cause, and you'll need time to determine the real issue. For example, the kid who yells "I hate you" actually doesn't hate you but does feel intense anger. Your job is to figure out why, with compassion, so you can help your kid manage those emotions constructively. As parents, we complicate matters when our own hurt feelings and anger inform our reactions. Hijacking your kids' issues and making them about you serves no good purpose. Instead, remain mindful so you can support your kid in learning how to handle the situation better.

Although many conflicts diffuse when parents refrain from escalation, some situations require a powerful response. If your child can't hear your words when you speak calmly, you may need to yell. But do so purposefully, because yelling is the most effective response available in the situation, and not because you can't control your own frustration or sheer reactive anger. Similarly, if you believe in spanking, do so only when your own emotions are fully in control—never, ever, hit a child out of rage. Pause and/or practice Sharing Compassion, and then decide what needs to be done. And do it, accountably.

Expressions of compassion can be gentle and soft, and they can be fierce and formidable. Compassionate responses reduce suffering by preventing greater harm. Giving a child a time out appropriately is an act of compassion. In contrast, allowing a child to act disrespectfully and without discipline is not compassionate. Those behavioral patterns lead to undesirable outcomes. Agreeing with your teenager on reasonable consequences for transgressions, and imposing them when warranted, is compassionate. Allowing your teenager to abuse your trust because you don't want to issue a reprimand is not kindness. Respectfully demanding a certain code of conduct effectively positions kids for easier, more successful lives. Failing to teach them how to have self-discipline is a set up for disaster.

MINDFUL OF ALL THAT'S GOOD

It's easy to focus on applying mindfulness to the challenges of parenting because the benefits are so obvious. However, mindfulness is equally as relevant—if not more so—in the context of the joys and successes that parenting brings. Noticing and affirming good behavior reinforces desirable outcomes in desirable ways.

Although well-intentioned, some parental actions create unhealthy patterns. The problem comes when parents focus excessively on correcting their kids' deficits and insufficiently on cultivating positive behaviors and qualities. Without mindfulness, it's easy to become fixated on outcomes and lose sight of the process.

Let's consider two of the most common approaches to giving normally well-behaved kids privileges like iPad time, watching TV, or going out on a weekend night. But regardless of approach, remember that parents need to outline expectations clearly so kids know what to do—and what not to do. Decide how to offer warnings, constructively, to remind kids of expectations. Also important is letting kids know about likely consequences of their behaviors, desirable or not.

The first approach involves offering kids privileges as incentives. So when the kid meets parental expectations, good things happen. In other words, *if* the child behaves, *then* he or she gets the treat. The driving idea here is that offering rewards leads kids to become "mindful" of their own behavior. Unfortunately, this approach rarely works, and promoting mindful behavior as a way to earn privileges suggests that there's a prize for practicing mindfulness. It also promotes constant anxiety for a child who subsequently wonders, "Am I good enough?"

The second approach assumes that the child has already learned how to act responsibly and otherwise behave constructively. Thus privileges are not "special" but a given. If the kid messes up, then he or she loses those privileges for a reasonable period of time. The outcome is not a surprise, and the strategy normalizes desirable behavior through giving children a measure of control. Their behavior determines whether they keep privileges or lose them.

Cultivate mindfulness so you can celebrate and strengthen your children's growth. Pay attention to their successes at least as much as, if not more than, the ways in which they seem to fall short. Model compassion and demonstrate constructive behaviors.

Parent them the way you want them to parent their own children, which may or may not be consistent with the way your parents raised you. The idea is to parent proactively for the future (your childrens and their childrens) rather than parent reactively to the way you were parented in the past.

Above all, have patience. Almost all the trials of parenting pass with time and usually resolve acceptably if not desirably. Learning takes time, and we all make mistakes. We are responsible for keeping our children safe, and we are also responsible for allowing them to learn through trial and error within a safe environment. Parenting can be tremendously joyful and unbearably painful, although most of the time raising kids is an ongoing experience of hard work made meaningful by profound love. Practicing mindfulness maximizes the highs and eases the lows of parenting, just as it helps with the highs and lows of all experience. As we'll explore in the next chapter, sometimes all you can do is get through the day, and even (especially) then, applying mindfulness and Sharing Compassion can make all the difference.

11 • Mindfulness in the Midst of Pain

IN THE PREVIOUS chapter, we focused on applying mindfulness to parenting and touched on many of the major life changes, challenges, and joys associated with having and raising children—which, despite its difficulties, is generally an optimistic venture. Each child is a new life, replete with promise; barring calamity, the future holds opportunity. This essentially hopeful framework supports parents through the challenges and pain of childrearing. The pleasure of raising children also returns adults to the ever-opening landscape of childhood, but with greater appreciation and mental sophistication—a joyful, fulfilling experience.

In contrast, practicing mindfulness in the midst of physical and emotional pain, such as during illness and injury or at the end of life, heightens our very human awareness of the ever-narrowing horizon of our lives. And if we get stuck in the pain, or are moving toward the end of all pain, the process often seems beyond our control—a feeling that destabilizes us further. Sometimes the only thing left to do is just get through the pain, horror, or heartbreak. Mild or acute, we survive pain second by second, minute by minute, until something changes.

The experience of pain triggers mental, emotional, and physical responses. These changes take a toll, exacerbating the present situation and often leading to more pain in the future. As explored in detail earlier in this book, too much emotional stress, for too long, can have profound effects on your mental and physical health. Though the normal stress response (associated with "fight or flight") might help you extricate yourself from a dangerous situation, it does not relieve physical discomfort or emotional distress. Instead, a sustained experience of stress weakens resilience. Practicing mindfulness, on the other hand, offers a constructive strategy for acknowledging, managing, and if possible reducing pain.

Meditation may also reduce some of the undesirable experiences associated with anticipating pain.

If you worry in advance, you're likely to build up the expectation of pain—and consequently feel greater pain than you would otherwise experience. Just think about what happens when you get an injection. If you fear the needle and worry about the pain, you'll tense up around the injection site, which can make it hurt more. You may even flinch, and the injection might not go smoothly.

Instead, staying present with the your body means you only experience what's actually happening now. Pain hurts, no doubt about it. But pain is just pain, and it almost always eventually passes. Fearing or expecting pain is counterproductive: doing so imposes a possible and undesirable future outcome on the present. This informs, as well as prolongs, the actual experience of pain.

Now picture what happens when your kid gets an injection. If you manage your anxiety, it's easier to engage (if not distract) your child until he or she notices that the injection is in process. By that point, the worst is over, and your child has already experienced the discomfort. In contrast, if you nervously reassure your child that "it won't hurt too much," your association between injection and pain may well prime your child to scream as soon the nurse appears with a syringe.

Vigorous wriggling frequently follows such screaming, and when kids struggle, they tense up. In this way, anticipating future discomfort can cause your child unnecessary mental pain in advance of the event, as well as even greater physical pain. Additionally, you—the parent— experience double distress: your own and your child's. Although you cannot control your child's direct response to getting an injection, your mindfulness can certainly influence the experience.

Mindfulness techniques do not dull your senses or promote distraction and denial. Rather, they guide your attention into direct contact with *whatever is happening* so you can live your experience, intimately, and find solace while staying present.

Pain is pain: it remains either until something happens to you (such as medical treatment or the passage of time) or something happens within you (for instance, you train your mind). Either way, the challenge is to live with *what is* even as you use constructive options to manage and alleviate your pain. Do not substitute mindfulness for appropriate mainstream interventions. Instead, work with your mind to enhance everything else you can do for your brain and body. This chapter explains how.

When You Hurt

There are two general types of pain: physical and emotional. Of these, physical pain is the least complicated because *something tangible* hurts, either temporarily or chronically. Extreme pain, even if temporary, can be all-consuming. Chronic pain, no matter the degree, can overshadow other realms of experience. For many people, pain is a constant companion that never fully leaves, but even this pain becomes easier to bear with mindfulness.

Emotional pain can be just as overwhelming, and unfortunately, it's often followed by physical pain. Consider the last time you experienced deep sorrow, loss, or disappointment. Did the pain remain abstract in your mind, or did your body mirror your feelings? Did physical pain, in the form of aches, illness, or even sleeplessness, provide a more tangible reminder of psychic agony? Maybe your body stays strong through the crux of an emotional crisis only to collapse afterward. Or perhaps you only realize the depth of your mental anguish when a headache forces you to acknowledge the pain in your mind. Although each person has a unique set of responses to different types of pain, all of us experience pain on multiple levels.

The inextricable connections between brain and body ensure that pain, whatever its source, saturates other systems. What we refer to as the "mind" arises from the chemical workings of the brain, which can trigger physical as well as emotional and mental responses. Happiness, sadness, and pain are experienced at the physical level. And the experience of the body likewise influences the brain. But just as this web of interconnections causes pain to radiate, so too does it support multiple opportunities for managing pain, or at least reducing its toll.

Physical Pain

The experience of physical pain is the best place to begin exploring the effect of mindfulness on pain management; although physical suffering involves a multifaceted set of responses, it's less psychologically complex than emotional anguish. Consider what happens when your finger is crushed in a car door:

1) Your finger HURTS.
2) You do something active to try to mitigate the pain: perhaps you pull your finger away from door, grab it with your other hand, put it in your mouth, or rush off to run it under cold water. You also might start moving, maybe jumping from foot to foot or shimmying your torso, as if to run away from the pain.
3) You begin to feel strong emotions even as your crushed finger stings, throbs, and aches.
4) You unleash a verbal torrent of distress or anger.
5) Once the pain recedes somewhat, your analytical mind begins to seek some type of explanation for what happened and, if possible, assign fault.

You're likely to move through this sequence rapidly once your mind can focus on something other than the pain in your finger. After the last step, your emotions might shift as you become annoyed with yourself (if it was your fault) or furious with someone else (if it was theirs). A crushed finger, therefore, can easily lead to a major argument, deeply hurt feelings, and words that, once spoken, cannot be taken back.

So what can you do? Here are a few suggestions. (But, of course, also be sure to seek medical attention and ensure your health and safety.)

1) Your finger HURTS.

a. Take a long deep breath, and if possible shift your attention to the inhalation and exhalation. Do this again and again until you can tolerate the pain. This has two benefits:

    i. Deep breathing supports your brain's efforts to restore some kind of balance in your system, despite the injury, and helps mitigate the byproducts of a sustained stress response.

    ii. Shifting your attention from the pain to your breath requires focus and discipline, but it will decrease your perception of the intensity of the pain and also reinforce the reality that *you are more than the pain in your finger.*

b. Get to know your pain. Perhaps this sounds crazy, but if you cannot escape the pain the best alternative is to go into it more deeply. Notice its qualities and how it changes. Stay with it purposefully, rather than allowing it to hold your focus. Sometimes moving more deeply into the pain actually makes it more bearable because you see *that it does change.*

2) You do something active to try to mitigate the pain.

a. Continue breathing steadily to support your body.

b. Focus on noticing what your body is doing. You might even wonder, "Why am I hopping up and down?" or "How come shaking my hand seems to dull the pain?"

    Such spontaneous movements serve to distract your brain from the sensation of pain in your finger. If you stay perfectly still, the pain in your finger will metaphorically overwhelm your entire body. However, moving your body triggers other sensations that require management by the brain, which, in turn, help keep your finger's sensations in perspective.

3) You begin to feel strong emotions.

a. Notice your emotions as they arise, and keep breathing.

b. Recognize that they are triggered by pain and therefore colored by context.

c. Watch to see which emotions arise without pursuing or reinforcing any, and then let them pass on their own. In other
words, allow different emotions to appear and disappear
without engaging with them.

Emotions are like lightening in the sky during a storm:
they flash and attract your attention, then disappear in the
darkness. Even if they strike forcefully, you can ground the
energy of emotions by remaining mindful. Without mindfulness, such energy can carry and scorch.

4) You unleash a verbal torrent of distress or anger.
   a. Notice the words as they initially form in your mind or as
      you utter them.
   b. Remember that words carry the energy of physical *and* emo-
      tional feelings and that the propulsion of strong feelings is
      likely to impact others.
   c. Manage your words and sounds as best you can.
   d. Try to stop or temper destructive words; they will only lead
      to more pain of a different sort.
      i. If you feel anger, notice whether you want to (or actually
         start to) yell or swear at something or someone. Consider
         that allowing your pain to let you make others suffer is
         not moral or kind.
      ii. If you feel annoyance, you might yell or swear at yourself.
          But why? You're already hurt... and beating up on your-
          self for having a crushed finger (even if you accidently
          slammed the car door on yourself) serves no constructive
          purpose.

5) You seek some type of explanation for what happened and, if
   possible, assign fault.
   a. Watch your thoughts—both their content and the sequence
      in which they arise—so you can consider whether you're
      assigning blame accurately or inaccurately.

      If you blame someone else for your own mindlessness,
      you multiply the pain that pervades the situation. You can-

not magically heal your hurt finger, but you can refrain from making other things worse.

b. Take appropriate action. If someone thoughtlessly slammed the door on you, for instance, by all means hold that person accountable but do so constructively—so they (and everyone else present) will be more likely to look first in the future.

Ultimately, the challenge is to find some way to accept that your finger hurts and move forward to help it heal, whether that means putting ice on it or going to the ER. Physical pain is undesirable, but it's just pain. It will pass, or at least change. Until it does, keep breathing.

Emotional Pain

The process of applying mindfulness to pure emotional pain involves a shorter sequence of steps than working with physical pain. However, the context of working with emotional pain is frequently more complicated and challenging. Whereas physical pain derives from tangible reality, emotional pain is abstract and therefore harder to recognize as a distinct experience. In other words, using your mind to focus on a crushed finger is much easier than using your stressed mind to recognize its own distress.

In addition, although your suffering does not have a physical cause, it often *becomes* physical. Searing nonphysical pain can literally "take your breath away" and pervade your body. Muscles can cramp, you might vomit, your heart might feel tight or flutter or race. Although you can—and should—treat physical symptoms, they are likely to continue until the other, deeper, invisible pain eases. This means working with your mind to produce desirable changes in your brain that, in turn, benefit your mind and overall well-being.

The problem is that the mind is both the source and solution to the pain that it experiences, and focusing your mind when in mental distress is no easy feat. Your mind must notice the pain, identify its cause, recognize how mindfulness practice can help you manage (and hopefully reduce) the pain, sustain the capacity to apply mindfulness, and do so for as long as necessary. These actions are subtle and strenuous, and difficult to implement without prior training—which is precisely why regular mindfulness practice is so important. The idea is that you train to the point where applying mindfulness becomes second nature and you feel confident about your ability to remain mindful, even under great duress. Imagining yourself in the situations below can facilitate understanding how to practice mindfulness in horribly painful circumstances:

- **Your ten-year-old child develops a severe illness that goes undiagnosed, and therefore untreated, for many months.** During that time period, you watch your bright and strong child deteriorate mentally and physically. The suffering is even more pronounced because of the uncertainty. As you pursue every available medical option, you start to wonder whether your child will ever get better. You fear the loss of potential that you previously took for granted. All the while, you try to comfort your child and other family members. Sometimes the sheer terror and feelings of helplessness threaten to overwhelm you. You are doing everything possible, but you find no solace.

  At this point, the only thing left to do is remain resilient so you can continue your search for answers and sustain your ability to comfort your child. When your mind screams silently, switch your attention to breathing. When you hold your suffering child, crying invisibly within yourself, practice Sharing Compassion—for yourself, your child, and for the other friends and family members who suffer along with you. When you feel panic because yet another doctor lacks answers, breathe and notice that your thoughts are simply thoughts, lacking substance. Remember that the search continues, and focus on the process until you reach the answers. When your heart feels broken, keep breathing to stay present in the love you hold for your child—that shared connection gives rise to comfort and hope.

- **You're in an accident that leaves you bedridden for weeks,**

struggling with constant pain. You take medicine for relief when the pain is too intense, but you try not to use much because the painkillers make you drowsy and dull. There's not much you can do physically, other than get through the days while your body heals. Emotionally, you feel awful: worn down by the pain, depressed by the process of recovery, angry about the accident, worried about the consequences of your injuries, and frustrated about feeling so helpless. Initially, you distract yourself as much as possible, but then you realize that nothing out there can solve the disquiet within.

Recognize that although your body is inactive, your mind can move. This means you can train it. Practice mindfulness techniques that promote physical rest and thereby support greater healing. Turn your attention inward, and focus on your physical sensations day by day, becoming increasingly aware of your own body. Notice your thoughts; when they detour into unproductive regions, gently shift your attention to the present and return your attention to watching the travels of your mind. Recognize when your emotions inform your speech and actions, and be gentle with yourself and those who try to help you. Practice Sharing Kindness, and see if you experience some pleasure in extending the hope for happiness to others.

■ **Your coworker accuses you of creating a hostile work environment because you dissented respectfully and that person's ego cannot tolerate criticism of any type.** The complaint triggers a workplace review, and the system fails to distinguish between genuine abuse and personal vindictiveness. Your much-deserved promotion is derailed, and you miss a much-hoped-for opportunity. Although you're eventually cleared of any wrongdoing, your anger and resentment continue to fester. You hate going to work, even though you love the job and you feel good about what you do. Your unhappiness distracts you and detracts from everything else, and your quality of life suffers. Falling asleep is difficult, and you frequently wake up in the middle of the night as your mind spins, recycling the situation. As it continues, you feel even worse because you cannot stop toxic emotions from rippling outward and poisoning your life.

Recognize that your coworker's actions hit you hard and that the process of clearing your name is always bruising. Your anger and resentment are natural, but once acknowledged, they serve no further constructive purpose. You clearly did not ask for this experience, but you have to deal with its reality. This means you need to use your mind to discipline your thoughts and feelings. When the thoughts of unfairness, retribution, fury, and disappointment cycle, notice them and switch your attention to breathing, to noticing physical sensations, or to Sharing Compassion. When anger tightens your chest, breathe to allow your body to return to a resting state. When your attention wanders from the task at hand, reliving the past or imagining the future, return your focus to the present. Count breaths backward from twenty-one down toward zero to fall asleep, because allowing your body to rest will help you restore pleasure in your life. You can also practice sharing kindness with yourself and toward others, and even (eventually) toward your coworker. Considering that suffering less and feeling happier promotes more constructive behaviors, so that the strategy of extending compassion and kindness benefits everyone.

- **Your marriage ends when your spouse informs you "it's over."** Your brain is so overwhelmed that you cannot think clearly, and your emotions range from fury to grief, disappointment to disbelief. You feel the impulse to fight back, and then suddenly, you want to run away and hide. Your rational mind is missing in action, and your emotions drive your behavior. The situation is fraught with emotional risk and the potential for physical danger. You feel like your world is imploding and everything you relied on is dissolving. You have no idea what to do next.

All you can do, in those first shattering moments, is survive without creating more devastation. This means feeling intense emotions and managing them so you reduce your risks, emotionally and physically. Notice them, feel them, and stay with them; do not act on them, at least not yet. The same applies for the words that well up inside you. Focus on breathing to slow the stress response, and then continue to clear your mind. Later, breathe so your body and brain can rest. Pause before you unleash righteous anger. Hold yourself present in that moment, and allow time to return to its normal pace before you take action. Then, whatever you choose to do in response, continue to notice that your emotions are emotions: they will morph over time, arise and disappear. This way, your rational mind can benefit from the presence of your feelings without losing control.

■ **Your beloved spouse (or partner, parent, child, friend...) dies.** You're stunned by the loss. No one can help mitigate your pain, and you wonder whether you can recover. Nothing seems to matter, and your world becomes a wasteland.

Aside from seeking spiritual, medical, or other conventional and appropriate supports, there's not much you can do other than allow time to heal you—even if you cannot imagine that healing is possible. The immediate challenge lies in getting through each day, so that time actually does pass. Since thinking and feeling hurts, switch your attention to breathing, eating, walking, and sleeping. Wait, remaining focused on the present, and allow this moment to change over time, and thereby allow time to pass. Notice when you begin to see or hear or otherwise experience things just as they are, without thoughts, interpretations, or emotions. Slowly, rediscover your world and return to life.

SHARING COMPASSION WITH OTHERS

Sometimes the best way to alleviate your own suffering is to focus on someone else.

In structure, the practice of Sharing Compassion with Others is quite similar to Sharing Kindness; the idea is to generate and extend the desire for suffering to ease, if not end. You already know how to send yourself compassion, and in chapter 10, you learned how to extend compassion toward a child. Now consider broadening the focus of the practice even further, sending your feelings outward first toward a neutral acquaintance, then to someone you mildly dislike or find annoying, and eventually to someone you deeply dislike or toward whom you feel intense anger or even hatred. Go slowly without forcing yourself; the practice is only constructive if you can experience extending compassion generously and without internal resistance. Here are the instructions for **Sharing Compassion with Others**:

- **Focus your attention** on experiencing compassion and extending compassion from your heart toward another person.
- **Observe with awareness** whether you stay focused on experiencing and extending compassion to the other person, or whether you become distracted.
- **Refocus your attention**, if needed.

Although challenging, generating compassion for another in the midst of heartbreak is one of the most powerful ways to help yourself (and others). Maybe this seems unreasonably difficult; after all, how can a broken heart find the energy to extend caring to anyone else? I know heartbreak hurts. But staying in the pain, maybe to punish yourself or because you feel entitled to it, serves no constructive purpose. Remember that another person's suffering does not diminish your own. Instead, share compassion with others and, through doing so, extend compassion to yourself.

MINDFULNESS AT THE END OF LIFE

Mindfulness is a useful practice whether you're a caregiver of someone whose life is ending or if you're dying yourself. And either way, you can prepare in advance by cultivating mindfulness throughout your life. In the face of death, no matter your position, it's best to remain present, allow the mind and body to rest, experience the greatest possible mental clarity, and remain aware of compassion along with kindness.

Although death is inevitable, few of us spend much time or energy preparing for our own passing—or another's. However, contemplating death with mindfulness is a powerful practice in the here and now as well as good training for what is to come. When we're fortunate, the end of life approaches slowly and openly, giving time for preparation. If you know someone you love is dying, you can consider how best to ease the process—for yourself and your beloved. You might meditate on the inevitability of this person's death and practice noticing the thoughts and feelings that arise. This way, you gain familiarity with your own emotional and mental responses. When the end comes for a beloved, you will feel everything, vividly and acutely, but your feelings will not catch you by surprise. You will be more resilient and better able to remain present to the process.

By definition, there is no specific, contextual preparation for anyone's violent or unexpected death. But you can build the emotional resilience that will support you when the unexpected happens by contemplating the experience of death. You might feel even more alive as you increasingly accept the presence of death in life. This means learning to rest more easily with the knowledge that every living being must die. It also means coming to terms with the reality that another person's death can impact you—and even for the rest of your life.

At the end of someone else's life, there is very little left to do beyond saying whatever is left to say and providing physical, emotional, and spiritual comfort both for the living and the dying. Staying present with the dying person is an expression of profound compassion, and this means remaining *truly* present rather than busying yourself with the distractions that surround death. There will be time for making arrangements later, so the priority is to remain still even as someone slides into the end. You can speak gently and kindly, or you can remain silent.

Whether you speak or act or simply offer silent company, you can practice Sharing Compassion—for the other person's benefit as well as your own comfort. If the dying person wants to be touched, then reach out. If not, then do not impose. If the dying person is calm, make every effort to mirror that calmness and refrain from disrupting it with your own distress. As death nears, the dying person's state of mind should take priority; after the death, the focus switches back to the living. As much as possible, allow the dying person to remain dignified and present through the final transition.

If you're the person whose life is ending, pay attention to what you need and want—assuming that you're aware of what's happening. After all, although death is inevitable, the circumstances are uncertain; you cannot influence the circumstances of your death if it comes unexpectedly or when you're unconscious or asleep. But if your death comes slowly and you have time to prepare, notice what you think and feel, and reflect on what can help you pass as comfortably as possible. If you're able, give directions to your caregivers. This is a gift for them, because there is comfort in knowing that the help they provide is the help you desire. It's also important, critically important, for you to find comfort in knowing that your end of life will be aligned with how you have lived.

Preparing for your death can begin long before you reach the actual process of dying. Practicing mindfulness can help you reflect on death somewhat dispassionately, so you can explore your thoughts and feelings with relative calmness and clarity. Contemplating death is not necessarily morbid. Rather, recognizing that life is precious and limited can support experiencing daily life with far greater vibrancy and awareness. Considering death, in advance, can also help alleviate some of the anxiety and fear that comes with approaching such a significant event without preparation—even as it opens you to the bittersweet quality of love and loss. It can be of great value to include as part of your mindful relationship talking about the reality of death—and the reality that in all likelihood, one partner will die before the other. If that happens, what can you say now to your partner that will help her or him meet that reality? Giving mindful care to that reality can deepen love, connection, and even a sense of security.

In addition, consider writing a personal statement or letter to your loved ones that expresses the thoughts and feelings you would hope to share on your deathbed—none of us can be certain that we will have the opportunity when the time comes. This statement or letter can be anything you want: highly personal or public, specific to certain individuals or general. The process of writing such a document is both liberating and heart-wrenching. It can be excruciatingly painful to imagine leaving your loved ones, home, possessions, and daily experiences, and at the same time tremendously enriching to feel a sense of gratitude for all that you know, feel, and have. Once written, seal the document in an envelope, attach instructions regarding when to open it and read the contents, and give it (or copies of it) to your intended recipients. If you have a will, held in safety by a lawyer, you might also consider leaving a copy of this document in the care of the lawyer. That way, you have assurance that—at the very least—your loved ones will read document when they also learn the contents of your will. Remember that you live on in the minds and hearts of all who remember you, and sharing your thoughts and feelings in this manner can be your final gift.

You might also find comfort in expressing specific wishes regarding death and funeral particulars. At a minimum, create a living will and make any other appropriate legal arrangements regarding end-of-life care.

Death, too, is part of living mindfully.

It Ain't Necessarily So

Applying mindfulness to the experience of pain frequently gives rise to unexpected insights. The transition from being consumed or defined by pain to knowing that you can witness your experience of pain *in the moment* is life changing. This is an existential shift of self-identity, and it's a one-way street. Once you realize that *you are more than your pain*, you can never again be defined solely by pain. This transformation certainly reduces psychic discomfort, and it can also lessen the impact of physical pain. It's easier to live with pain when there's more to being alive than the pain.

Unfortunately, suffering precedes this transition. Healthy people rarely opt for increased pain in order to facilitate self-growth. We hope to avoid suffering, and we carry on until pain appears without invitation. At that point, we deal with it as reality.

This is not to say that the opportunity for transformation that comes with surviving incredibly difficult and painful experiences somehow justifies or explains why terrible things happen. I do not believe there is a grand purpose to the horror and heartbreak that people live through. But I do believe that we can try to make the best of truly terrible circumstances—the only alternative is worse.

As you practice mindfulness, you're likely to develop an increased familiarity with the way your mind spins stories and adds meanings to bare facts. It's useful to notice when your interpretations make something *unpleasant* into something truly *unbearable*. It's never nice when an intimate relationship ends, but it doesn't have to feel like the end of the world. Even in the worst of circumstances, our understanding and response to facts either mitigates or amplifies the pain.

Each of us is at the center of limitless concentric circles that spread outward and overlap with others. When we experience joy, we send it rippling through our relationships. This inevitably stimulates joy in others, and the waves continue far beyond our comprehension. The same is true for pain. My pain impacts everyone with whom I interact, from my loved ones who suffer with me to the person who sees my scowl while walking on the street. The chain of causes and consequences continues endlessly.

I believe that a life well lived generates more constructive energy than destruction. It's a matter of proportion, and I aspire for a ratio that favors positive contribution. This perspective is easier to uphold when things go well, and suffering is minimal. It's far more difficult when pain is a day-after-day experience. But even then, living *mindfully* with the pain is preferable—at multiple levels—to accepting that pain dominates my life.

Mindfulness is not a panacea. In some ways, practicing mindfulness actually brings you into more direct contact with pain, albeit with less fear and greater resilience. As you become increasingly compassionate, you're likely to recognize a more pervasive need for compassion, but you'll also have the capacity to respond accordingly. You won't feel less pain when you see other people suffering; in fact, you might feel that pain more acutely. However, knowing and encountering it without filters somehow makes it more bearable because you know what it is—and what it isn't.

Conclusion:
Mindfulness Now and for the Future

ONCE OUTSIDE THE WOMB, each human life begins with an inhalation. From then on, breathing supports life until that one last exhalation presages our final transition. To breathe is to live, and mindfulness techniques facilitate and sustain this realization. You know this through your past experience, reading, and practice. You also know that practicing mindfulness, like the act of breathing, is a lifelong endeavor. Wherever you are in your practice, there is more yet to come. It's a nonlinear progression that deepens multidimensionally over time.

In this book, we've journeyed through mindful living at different levels. We've trained in on-the-ground techniques and specific applications for mindfulness. We've also looked at the landscape of mindfulness from a distance; we've examined pain and suffering in some of the deepest valleys and also the high peaks of joy and compassion. We started with developing mindfulness for inner growth, but we quickly carried the benefits of the practice into relationships.

We took two basic approaches: applying mindfulness to promote optimal experience and, at the same time, training the mind to minimize harm. The absolute practice of mindfulness is essentially value-free, so we are ultimately responsible for imbuing mindfulness with meaning and direction. Developing mindfulness with the intention of promoting positive outcomes offers the journey of a lifetime; the horizons are limitless.

FROM THE BEGINNING TO THE PRESENT

Together we've woven a web of mindfulness techniques and applications. We've done this together, you and I, by combining the words in this book with your unique experience. In the beginning, my intention was to guide you to recognize your own path. By midbook, my focused shifted to facilitating your explorations. Now, in the last chapter, we became companions in our commitment to mindful living.

The practice of mindfulness reinforces the message that *what each of us does matters immensely*, for us individually, in relation to others, and in the world. Mindful living means realizing your optimal potential. The implications are vast and last a lifetime. However, the practice of mindfulness remains rooted in paying attention and deepening awareness of the little things.

Staying present means being here *now*, which is why mindfulness is both process and outcome. Just consider the process and outcome of reading this book. We began with preparation for Mindful Breathing; we explored taking a Mindful Breath, and we followed that by using Pause. As your attention and awareness sharpened, we experimented with body posture, seeking a stable and comfortable position that supports laser-like focus by reducing physical distractions.

Next we applied mini-mindfulness techniques to help manage and reduce the undesirable effects of that most insidious modern plague: stress. Unlike other approaches to stress, mindfulness promotes physiological rest while training the mind to become increasingly alert. Just as there are triggers for stress, so too is Mindful Breathing a trigger for allowing the body and mind to return to a resting or "ready" state. Therefore, we focused on the sensations of breathing while practicing Mindful Breathing, the book's first formal technique. With each repetition, we distilled the essential steps of practicing mindfulness into three core steps: focus, observe, and refocus.

From there, we shifted the focus of attention from the sensation of breathing to counting cycles of complete breaths. Mindful Counting and Mindful Breathing involve the same physical action (breathing) but prioritize different areas of emphasis. Regardless of whether you preferred feeling sensations to counting (or vice versa), you practiced focusing, observing, and refocusing. These are foundational techniques because they are simple and because they highlight the most basic experience of being alive. Paying attention to your breath both necessitates and facilitates staying present.

If we want to be truly, fully alive, we need to know both body and mind, so from breathing, we moved on to thinking as the object of attention. Many mindfulness practitioners, myself included, recall the "aha" experience of realizing that "there's more to me than my thoughts." There's a sense of freedom that comes with recognizing thoughts and feelings as mental events, rather than aspects of a permanent identity. Applying mindfulness to these mental events facilitates developing confidence in the constant presence of change. Since everything changes, all the time, remaining present is the only way to know what's actually happening in the here-and-now. Awareness of and in the current moment is the basis for making active choices about what we think, feel, say, and do. In contrast, mental absence puts us at the mercy of circumstances, others, and our familiar mental patterns.

Mindful Thinking and Mindful Feeling are intense and liberating techniques, but they can also be uncomfortable and, if practiced in isolation, distracting. It's easy to lose your orientation while wandering in the cerebral landscape of mental events. Staying centered, grounded with physical reality, helps maintain perspective. This is why we explored Mindful Listening, Mindfulness of Static Sensation, Stand with Attention, and Mindfulness of Dynamic Sensation next. The idea is to develop mindfulness of the body by training the mind, while knowing the mind through experience in the body.

Mindfulness and sex provides an attractive and relevant topic through which to tighten the connections between physical and mental activity. But Mindful Sex is multifaceted. Applying mindfulness to such intimate and loaded experience is challenging; it's also very real. From the relatively discrete topic of sex, we moved into broader but similarly complex applications: mindfulness in romantic as well as professional relationships. Sharing Kindness, in its many variations, is a natural outcome of mindfulness practice. Happiness is a present-moment experience, and wishing that other people experience joy is a profound act of generosity. Likewise, Sharing Compassion dedicates mindfulness to the intention and action of reducing suffering.

Accountability and compassion might seem to be the unlikeliest of partners, but they form a bridge that allows us to move toward a healthier shore. Each of us is accountable for what we think and say, as well as how we act. People make many good choices that contribute to community and the world, while enriching inner harmony. People also make grave mistakes and wreak damage through the consequences of destructive thoughts, speech, and actions. We have to be accountable for what we do, for better and for worse, and likewise, we can hope for compassion when we suffer through our own actions or at the hands of others. Compassion is not forgiveness; compassion does not "make everything all right again," but it seeks to alleviate the cause and results of suffering.

Kindness and compassion, joy and suffering, are the primary ingredients of mindful parenting. Being a parent is one of the most challenging, rewarding, and transformative of life experiences. Perhaps this is why it also provides one of the most powerful opportunities for practicing mindfulness—through the highs and the lows. Other significant opportunities include applying mindfulness to physical and emotional pain, as well as at the end of life.

If reading this book, and practicing the various included techniques, has been useful for you, it's because you used it to train your mind. Perhaps the book gave you a place to a start practicing mindfulness. Or maybe it contributed to your ongoing practice. Regardless, you are transforming the book's content into lived experience. You focused on mindfulness, observed your own experience, and refocused again. Ongoing reflection deepens practice, and so too does seeking further instruction.

FIND A TEACHER

Together, we've made our way here from chapter 1. But looking forward, I strongly encourage you to find authentic, skilled, and responsive teachers to support your practice. Books, with the disembodied voice of an author, are useful—but not enough. When you're ready, find a teacher who models what you want to learn. There are many teachers for many different students, and the fit between student and teacher is unique and personal. Recommendations from friends, family members, or colleagues are helpful, but not necessarily right for you. Also, be careful, because the demand for mindfulness training outreaches the availability of authentic teachers. Marvelous teachers exist, but there are also many charlatans. Always remember that you're in charge of your own practice.

Meditation is a journey: there are different guides and varied landscapes in which to practice. You can change where you go, and with whom. But it's best to approach change mindfully. Changing teachers simply to have variety is usually counterproductive. So too is developing a mix-and-match meditation practice. When you trust someone as an authentic teacher, have confidence in your decision and entrust that teacher with your practice. But never suspend your own judgment.

So what do you look for? And how will you know when you find a real teacher? Begin by watching, listening, learning, and questioning. Finding a meditation teacher is a little like buying a new house: you are preparing to entrust your precious mind into another person's safekeeping. Be patient and take due diligence seriously.

Here are some tips to help you consider whether you've found the right one. (Note: for the sake of convenience, I use the male pronoun "he" in the following discussion of teachers—but gender has nothing to do with being a good teacher.)

- **Do your research**. Attend teachings, read widely, and use media to learn from a variety of recognized and established meditation teachers. This will help you become familiar with the field and enrich your experience. Look for consistency, and recognize aberrations. I've studied with many different teachers, some for longer periods than others. There is always something to learn, either in the affirmative (because the teacher genuinely imparts wisdom) or by default (when the teacher isn't right, and you become more discerning in your search). Let your teachers earn your respect slowly: it's the only way to truly trust what they teach.

Your mind is your most precious asset, and just as mindfulness is both process and outcome, so too is studying with a teacher. The process is the purpose. This means you can apply mindfulness as you search for a teacher, and allow your teacher to demonstrate mindfulness in relation to you. All of my teachers offer the same advice repeatedly: "Students should always choose their teachers carefully, and good teachers are equally as careful in their choice of students."

A student's trust precedes the development of devotion, and both are essential for effective teaching. Authentic teachers want students to trust their instincts and intellectual assessment. Remember, if something feels or seems wrong about—or with—a teacher, it's better to assume that something is wrong. Likewise when the teacher-student fit feels right, and your critical assessment confirms your gut, then trust the process, and learn.

- **Remember that each of us can have many distinct but complementary teachers.** If you find a teacher who promises to "take you all the way" to some spiritual or mental destination—so long as you pledge total loyalty to his teachings—he probably isn't the real thing. Real teachers acknowledge authentic teachings and never censor their students' investigations to secure respect. My teachers all had multiple teachers of their own, and they naturally rejoice in the wisdom and skill of others. Good teachers do not need to be the only one. Although they might ask that you entrust them with your studies for a specific period of time, they would never bar you from other opportunities for learning during your lifetime. While it's much less confusing to study mental training intensively with one teacher at a time, you can certainly change your teachers over time.

■ **Consider a teacher's thoughts, speech, and actions as indications and outcomes of his own training.** Find out with whom he studied, and whether he devoted significant time to his own practice before becoming a teacher. Does he still devote time to his practice and continue to value his own teachers? These considerations apply regardless of whether a teacher takes a secular or spiritual approach. They are likewise relevant no matter your personal experience. Although more advanced students generally need teachers with greater depth and expertise, having a truly qualified teacher from the beginning will enhance your practice enormously.

Remember, we all follow the same trajectory with mindfulness practice; it's just that teachers started earlier and have enough experience to offer guidance to others. An authentic teacher will describe his training and background with confidence, gratitude, and humility. If a teacher boasts about studying with wise and famous teachers, he or she clearly didn't learn much from their teachings. This sounds cynical, but it's important to keep in mind, especially when you find a potential teacher with enormous charisma who spins a story of a star-studded past.

■ **Notice if a teacher's life models the practice of mindfulness.** Observe a teacher, both during formal teaching time and when the spotlight is off. Watch what he does and listen to what he says and how he says it. Look for alignment between the "talk" and the "walk."

I am frequently astonished by the simple kindness of my teachers' actions even in everyday life. They say "thank you" and appreciate efforts on their behalf. They also like to laugh and enjoy life, and they recognize that too much severity and austerity are unhealthy. They are normal people with extraordinary minds.

Having "faith" in a teacher is foolish unless you determine that the teacher is truly trustworthy. Teachers are people just like us, and we are responsible for seeing them *as they are*. They are responsible for embodying the teachings and offering guidance.

- **Evaluate how a teacher frames mindfulness practice.** Authentic teachers recognize that developing mindfulness brings many benefits, but they know that becoming "mindful" is not the ultimate goal. I believe that the point of mindfulness training is to contribute to ethical life, not teach you to become a "better breather." If you share this belief, then search for a teacher who teaches about the mind to touch the heart.

  Look for consistency between the training techniques and larger applications. Always pay attention if a teacher proposes objects of attention that lead you toward self-satisfaction without emphasizing the importance of contributing constructively to community. If so, he is likely to be more interested in feeding his own ego than genuinely helping you with yours. Real teachers also understand that they cannot promise you anything other than to support you in your own practice.

- **Evaluate the quality of a teacher's compassion.** A teacher worthy of your trust remains focused on the connection between mindfulness and compassion and knows that compassion is not always warm and fuzzy. Sometimes my teachers are incredibly harsh, but never to elevate themselves or inflict pain. They simply are trying to impart wisdom *in the most effective manner for each unique student*. Forceful speech can be skillful when simplicity and gentleness fail to convey the message. In contrast, less skillful teachers frequently think that sweet behavior, even to the point of syrupiness, is the mark of true caring—but it isn't.

  The quality of compassion has a single purpose: to reduce suffering. Sometimes being nice is an expression of true compassion. But at other times, compassion appears as firmness or even fierceness. Compassion is what drives a parent to set limits on a child, so the child learns what to value and how to behave well. Compassion is what enables a lover to hold a symbolic mirror to her beloved's face and help him see what's there. Compassion is the basis for standing up to injustice and intervening to prevent someone else from doing harm. A compassionate teacher knows how to engage a student most effectively according to his needs.

Secular and spiritual mindfulness teachers are proliferating as mindfulness becomes increasingly popular. Some are experienced practitioners ready to share techniques and follow their own teachers' recommendations and example. It is a blessing to find such teachers, even just one, in your lifetime.

However, be alert to opportunistic charlatans who pretend to be trustworthy teachers. They may, in fact, be profoundly manipulative people who seek to profit from other people's neediness by parading as "certified" teachers of mindfulness. They exploit their own charisma and teach to feed their egos. At the very least, this is dangerous because charlatans reduce the likelihood that their students will have a positive experience with mindfulness. At worst, the potential for damaging abuse is very, very real.

The majority of new mindfulness teachers appear to be well-intentioned professionals from the fields of education, psychology, religion, and medicine. Many have a special ability to translate original teachings into a practical and modern approach accessible for secular and very busy people. However, don't automatically assume that you will get authentic mindfulness teachings from a nurse, therapist, or pastor who has years of experience in stress management—and took a mindfulness training course. The learning curve is steep and continuous, and teachers with insufficient experience can hit the same obstacles as their students. Be careful to whom you give your trust, and then be glad when you find a deserving teacher.

Although mindfulness meditation grew from Buddhist practice, most modern mindfulness teachers are not—and do not need to be—Buddhist. However, if you want to pursue Buddhist meditation, find an authentic Buddhist teacher. The same applies if you are drawn to the Christian practices of contemplative prayer or hunger for meditation as taught in mystical Judaism, Islam, or any other wisdom tradition. Likewise, if a secular mindfulness practice calls you, you can find and trust mindful teachers who lead ethical lives. No matter the tradition, the practice of honoring authentic teachers and teachings is universal. Likewise, the joy of studying and deepening your practice has no bounds.

RIGHT HERE, RIGHT NOW

Mindfulness is an experiential practice. Although mediated by concepts and expressed through words, the essence of mindfulness practice is nonverbal and nonconceptual. It is simply about being fully and compassionately present: using your mind to know your mind, and honoring the experience of your heart and body. A momentary practice that spans a lifetime, mindfulness is a solo journey that nevertheless relies on teachers and companions. As we've explored in this book, training in formal techniques prepares us to apply mindfulness informally.

Over the past chapters, you have given me the privilege of encouraging your exploration. Now as this book ends, your personal practice begins anew. Mindful living is the experience of practicing mindfulness as a way of life. This is our birthright as human beings. The point is being right here, right now. I am confident that you know how.

Acknowledgments

We are grateful for the assistance of many people, including Laura Cunningham (our superb editor), Josh Bartok (for the gift of his vision and skill *in the beginning and at the end*), and the team at Wisdom Publications, as well as Janet Corkins and Ethan Joel Guerry.

We especially appreciate the generous support of Charles Goldstein and Leslie Jeffs Senke, who gave so much of their precious time, attention, and advice.

As always, we remain deeply grateful for the wisdom of our teachers. Their blessings made this book possible.

References

Brown, C. A., & Jones, A. K. P. (2010). Meditation experience predicts less negative appraisal of pain: Electrophysiological evidence for the involvement of anticipatory neural responses. *PAIN, 150,* 428–38. htttp://dxdoi.org/10.1016/j.pain.2010.04.017

Carmondy, J., & Baer, R. A. (2008). Relationships between mindufflness practice and levels of mindfulness, medical and psychological symptoms and well-being in a mindfullness-based stress reduction program. *Journal of Behavioral Medicine, 31*(1), 23–33. http://dxdoi.org/10.1007/s/10865-007-9130-7

Chambers, R., Lo, B. C. Y., & Allen, N. B. (2008). The impact of intensive mindfulness training on attentional control, cognitive style, and affect. *Cognitive Therapy and Research, 32*(3), 303–22. http://dx.doi.org/10.1007/s10608-007-9119-0

Chiesa, A., & Serretti, A. (2009). Mindfulness-based stress reduction for stress management in healthy people: A review and meta-analysis. *The Journal of Alternative and Complementary Medicine, 15*(5), 593–600. http://dxdoi.org/10.1089=acm.2008.0495

Chiesa, A., & Serretti, A. (2011a). Mindfulness based cognitive therapy for psychiatric disorders: A systematic review and meta-analysis. *Psychiatry Research, 187*(3), 441–53. http://dx.doi.org/10.1016/j.psychres.2010.08.011

Chiesa, A., & Serretti, A. (2011b). Mindfulness-based interventions for chronic pain: A systematic review of the evidence. *Journal of Alternative & Complementary Medicine, 17*(1), 83.

Crum-Cianflone, N. F., Bagnell, M. E., Schaller, E., Boyko, E. J.,

Smith, B., Maynard, C.,... Smith, T. C. (2014). Impact of combat deployment and posttraumatic stress disorder on newly reported coronary heart disease among US active duty and reserve forces. *Circulation, 129*(18), 1813–20. http://dxdoi.org/10.1161/CIRCULATIONAHA.113.005407

Davidson, R. J., Kabat-Zinn, J., Schumacher, J., Rosenkranz, M., Muller, D.l, Santorelli, S. F.,... Sheridan, J. F. (2003). Alterations in brain and immune function produced by mindfulness meditation. *Psychosomatic Medicine, 65*(4), 564–70. http://dxdoi.org/10.1097/01.PSY.0000077505.67574.E3

Ekman, P. (2004). *Emotions revealed: Recognizing faces and feelings to improve communication and emotional life.* New York, N.Y.: Henry Holt and Co.

Epel, E. S., Blackburn, E. H., Jue, L., Dhabhar, F. S., Adler, N. E., Morrow, J. D., & Cawthon, R. M. (2004). Accelerated telomere shortening in response to life stress. *Proceedings of the National Academy of Sciences of the United States of America, 101*(49), 17312–315.

Felitti, V. J., Anda, R. F., Nordenberg, D., Williamson, D. F., Spitz, A. M., Edwards, V.,... Marks, J. S. Relationship of childhood abuse and household dysfunction to many of the leading causes of death in adults. *American Journal of Preventive Medicine, 14*(4), 245–58. http://dxdoi.org/10.1016/S0749-3797(98)00017-8

Flook, L., Goldberg, S. B., Pinger, L., Bonus, K., & Davidson, R. J. (2013). Mindfulness for teachers: A pilot study to assess effects on stress, burnout and teaching efficacy. *Mind, Brain and Education, 7,* 182–95. http://dxdoi.org/10.1111/mbe.12026

Geary, C., & Rosenthal, S. L. (2011). Sustained impact of MBSR on stress, well-being, and daily spiritual experiences for 1 year in academic health care employees. *Journal of Alternative and Complementary Medicine, 17*(10), 939–44.

Gold, E., Smith, A., Hopper, L., Herne, D., Tansey, G., & Hulland, C. (2010). Mindfulness-based stress reduction (MBSR) for primary school teachers. *Journal of Child and Family Studies, 19,* 184–89. http://dxdoi.org/10.1007/s10826-009-9344-0

Goleman, D. (2006). *Emotional intelligence.* New York, NY: Bantam Books.

Heydenfeldt, J. A., Herkenhoff, L., & Coe, M. (2011). Cultivating mind fitness through mindfulness training: Applied neuroscience. *Performance Improvement, 50*(10). http://dxdoi.org/10.1002/pfi.20259

Hofmann, S. G., Sawyer, A. T., Witt, A. A., & Oh, D. (2010). The effect of mindfulness-based therapy on anxiety and depression: A meta analytic review. *Journal of Clinical Psychology, 78*(2), 169–83. http://dxdoi.org/10.1037/a0018555

Kozasa, E. H., Sato, J. R., Lacerda, S. S., Barreiros, M. A. M., Radvany, J., Russel, T. A,... Amaro Jr., E. (2012). Meditation training increases brain efficiency in an attention task. *NeuroImage, 59,* 745–49. http://dxdoi.org/10.1016/j.neuroimage.2011.06.088

Krasner, M. S., Epstein, R., M., Beckman, H., Suchman, A., Chapman, B., Mooney, C. J, & Quill, T. E. (2009). Association of an educational program in mindful communication with burnout, empathy, and attitudes among primary care physicians. *Journal of the American Medical Association, 302*(12), 1284–93.

Levine A. B., Levine L. M., Levine T. B. (2014). Posttraumatic stress disorder and cardiometabolic disease. *Cardiology, 127,* 1–19.

Levy, D. M., Wobbrock, J. O., Kaszniak, A. W., & Ostergren, M. (2012). *The effects of mindfulness meditation training on multitasking in a high-stress information environment.* Paper presented at the Graphics Interface Conference, Toronto, Ontario.

Luszczynska, A., Scholz, U., & Schwarzer, R. (2005). The general self-efficacy scale: multicultural validation studies. *Journal of Psychology, 139*(5), 439–57.

Lutz, A., Brefczynski-Lewis, J., Johnstone, T., & Davidson, R. J. (2008). Regulation of the neural circuitry of emotion by compassion meditation: Effects of meditative expertise. *PLoS ONE, 3*(3), e1897. http://dxdoi.org/10.1371/journal.pone.0001897

Lutz, A., Slagter, H., Rawling, N., Francis, A., Greischar, L. L., & Davidson, R. J. (2009). Mental training enhances attentional stability: Neural and behavioral evidence. *Journal of Neuroscience, 29*(42), 13418–27.

Oman, D., Shapiro, S. L., Thoresen, C. E., Plante, T. G., & Flinders, T. (2008). Meditation lowers stress and supports forgiveness among college students: A randomized controlled trial. *Journal of American College Health, 56*(5), 569–78.

Paulson, S., Davidson, R., Jha, A., & Kabat-Zinn, J. (2014). Becoming conscious: The science of mindfulness. *Annals of the New York Academy of Sciences, 1303*(87–104). http://dxdoi.org/10.1111/nyas.12203

Piet, J., & Hougaard, E. (2011). The effect of mindfulness-based cognitive therapy for prevention of relapse in recurrent major depressive disorder: A systematic review and meta-analysis. *Clinical Psychology Review, 31*(6), 1032–40.

Reiner, K., Tibi, L., & Lipsitz, J. (2012). Do mindfulness-based interventions reduce pain intensity? A critical review of the literature. *Pain Medicine,* Epub ahead of print. http://dxdoi.org/10.1111/pme.12006

Ricard, M. (2011). *The art of happiness.* New York: Atlantic Books Ltd.

Roberts, K. C., & Danoff-Burg, S. (2010). Mindfulness and health behaviors: Is paying attention good for you? *Journal of American College Health, 59*(3), 165–73.

Stanely, E. A., Schaldach, J. M., Kiyonaga, A., & Jha, A. P. (2011). Mindfulness-based mind fitness training: A case study of a high stress predeployment military cohort. *Cognitive and Behavioral Practice, 18*, 566–76.

Tang, Y. Y., Lu, Q., Fan, M., Yang, Y., & Posner, M. I. (2012). Mechanisms of white matter changes induced by meditation. *Proceedings of the National Academy of Sciences, 109*(26), 10570–10574.

van Leeuwen, S., Singer, W., & Melloni, L. (2012). Meditation increases the depth of information processing and improves the allocation of attention in space. *Frontiers in Human Neuroscience, 6* (Article 133), 1–16. http://dxdoi.org/10.1016/j.neuroimage.2011.07.008

About the Authors

Deborah Schoeberlein David, MEd, is an education consultant and mindfulness trainer. She has more than twenty-five-years' experience working with not-for-profit, educational and governmental organizations in the United States and abroad. She is the author of *Mindful Teaching and Teaching Mindfulness: A Guide for Anyone Who Teaches Anything* (Wisdom Publications, 2009). Deborah has been widely published in professional journals, trade magazines, and online. She is also a guest blogger on the *Huffington Post*.

David Panakkal, MD, is a practicing psychiatrist with thirty years of clinical and teaching experience. A retired Colonel, US Army Medical Corps, and former Director of Mental Health Services for the US Department of State, his work has spanned the globe. David utilizes mindfulness techniques in his clinical practice as well as in stress management training for law enforcement, military, and diplomatic service members.

About Wisdom Publications

To LEARN MORE about Wisdom Publications, a nonprofit publisher, and to browse our other books dedicated to skillful living, visit our website at wisdompubs.org/livingmindfully.

You may request a copy of our catalog online or by writing to this address:

Wisdom Publications
199 Elm Street
Somerville, Massachusetts 02144 USA
Telephone: 617-776-7416
Fax: 617-776-7841
Email: info@wisdompubs.org
wisdompubs.org

Wisdom is a nonprofit, charitable 501(c)(3) organization affiliated with the Foundation for the Preservation of the Mahayana Tradition (FPMT).

Also Available from Wisdom Publications

MINDFUL TEACHING AND TEACHING MINDFULNESS
A Guide for Anyone Who Teaches Anything
Deborah Schoeberlein David
Suki Sheth, PhD

"A gift for educators, helpful in any classroom, for any teacher and with every student."
—Goldie Hawn, children's advocate and founder of the Hawn Foundation

HOW TO WAKE UP
A Buddhist-Inspired Guide to Navigating Joy and Sorrow
Toni Bernhard

"This is a book for everyone."
—Alida Brill, author of *Dancing at the River's Edge*

MINDFULNESS IN PLAIN ENGLISH
Bhante Gunaratana

"A classic—one of the very best English sources for authoritative explanations of mindfulness."
—Daniel Goleman, author of *Emotional Intelligence*

The Grace in Aging
Awaken as You Grow Older
Kathleen Dowling Singh

"Don't grow old without it."
—Rachel Naomi Remen, MD, author of *Kitchen Table Wisdom*

Veggiyana
The Dharma of Cooking: With 108 Deliciously Easy Vegetarian Recipes
Sandra Garson

"*Veggiyana* is more than just a cookbook—it's a feast in itself.
It is a book to be treasured, living as it will in my kitchen and
in my heart."
—Toni Bernhard, author of *How to Be Sick*

Mindfulness Yoga
The Awakened Union of Breath, Body, and Mind
Foreword by Georg Feuerstein

A *Yoga Journal* Editor's Choice

Waking Up Together
Intimate Partnership on the Spiritual Path
Ellen Jikai Birx and Charles Shinkai Birx

"A tribute to splendid marriage, from wise and spirited guides."
—Raphael Cushnir, author of *Setting Your Heart on Fire*